Everyday Joy

Everyday Joy

365 Days of OhMyGod Life

Z Egloff and
Melissa Phillippe

An OhMyGod Life Publication

Everyday Joy: 365 Days of OhMyGod Life

© 2017 by OhMyGod Productions

All Rights Reserved

An OhMyGod Life Publication
www.OhMyGodLife.com
Santa Rosa, CA

Cover Art: Z Egloff
Cover Design: Ted Raess

ISBN 10 978-1976431326
ISBN 13 1976431328

Printed in the United States of America

Dedicated to the memory of Carolyn Hayes Phillippe

This is a book about joy. As such, we encourage you to take it lightly. If you want to read each entry on the proper day, first thing in the morning, feel free. If you want to open a random page from time to time, feel free. If you want to read the whole book, cover to cover, all at once, feel free. If you want to sit high atop a yak and recite this book to a flock of penguins (provided you find the cooperative components), feel free. You get the idea. *It's about joy.* And we all approach joy in our own ways.

Consider this page your *Get-Into-Joy-Free Card.*

In Joy,
Melissa + Z

January 1

New beginnings can be scary. They can also be exiting and invigorating. Today, I open to the new. What new ideas are calling me? What new inspirations are wanting to take shape in my life? As I listen, I allow my intuition to show me the first steps to take. These steps might feel daunting. But I am not alone. Spirit is here. In every step, in every breath, Spirit is with me.

I step into the new. I am safe.

January 2

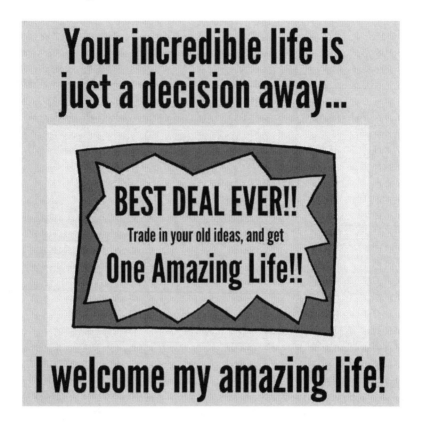

My mind is full of all sorts of thoughts. Some of them serve me very well. Others don't serve me at all. They *think* they do, but they don't! It's great to take inventory from time to time and clear out the thoughts that are no longer serving me. *Bye-bye, old thoughts!* You served me the best you could, but now you gotta go. The reward? A brand new life!

I release my outdated thoughts. I embrace my new life!

January 3

I am an awesome being. Even when I forget that this is true, it's still true. In fact, this is one of the awesome things about me. I'm awesome *all the time* – whether I know it or not! Today I remember that my awesomeness is always percolating inside me in the form of new ideas and inspirations. Who knows what I might come up with?! I am willing to be surprised!

I am constantly amazing myself. I am awesome!

January 4

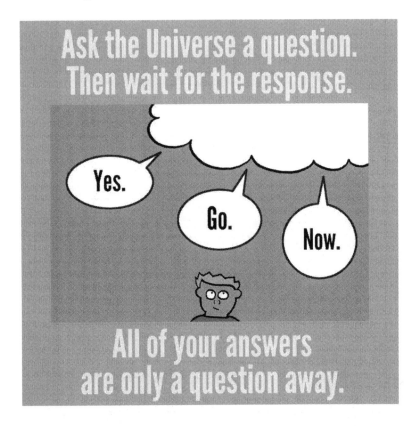

Whenever I ask the Universe a question, I always get an answer. It may not come in the form I'm expecting. I may not hear it at first. But I always get an answer. Sometimes the answer comes from a book. Or something someone says. Or an inner knowing. The more I ask, and the more answers I receive, the better I get at recognizing the answers when they arrive.

I am guided and supported by the Universe. Every day!

January 5

It's a good thing to be grateful, any time of day. But when I remember to be grateful at *night*, I sleep in the energy of gratitude all night long! So I count my blessings, including noticing those things I sometimes forget to be thankful for, things I take for granted. Like oxygen! I allow myself to fall asleep in this vibrational field of gratitude. It blesses my body and being. All. Night. Long.

I count my blessings tonight. Gratitude blesses my sleep.

January 6

When I was younger, I cared a lot more about what other people thought of me. The older I get, the less this is true. Not that I don't care about other people and what they think. Other people are fascinating! But their opinions about *me*? Not. My. Concern. Besides, most people are so wrapped up in their own lives, any opinion about *me* is really about *them*. What a wonderful realization!

I am free to be me.

January 7

There are so many amazing things in this world. All I have to do is look at the vast open beauty of the sky, or the joy of children playing, or the quiet peace of a forest. There are so many reminders of Spirit's presence in the world. When I get caught up in my own drama, I sometimes forget all about them. Today I remember to remember. I look. I listen. I am in awe.

I am open to awe, everywhere I find it.

January 8

When I think I'm confused, I let it awaken me. What am I resisting seeing? I muster my courage and look square into the face of what is mine to do (or not do). I understand that my inner knowing is Spirit guiding me. I am willing to take the next step in following this guidance because I trust Spirit. When I trust Spirit, life gets better and better.

I am willing to know what I know. I trust my inner guidance. The Divine has my back!

January 9

Sometimes the stresses of life build up inside me. That's when I know it's time to release a little steam. Finding ways to release my pent-up energy means that I don't have to take out my stress on others. After all, that would only lead to more stress! Instead, I release my built-up tension through my body, or my voice, or whatever works best for me. I always feel better afterwards.

I shake, rattle, and roll. Whoooooo Hoooooo!!!!

January 10

When someone does or says something I don't like, my first response may be to tell them what I think. But what if, when I find myself having an uncomfortable reaction to someone, I don't say anything at all? Sometimes silence is the best response for everyone – including myself. There are times when I *do* need to say something, but having silence in my repertoire makes me even more powerful.

I know what to say in every moment, including nothing.

January 11

Everyone has their own internal setting of lack or abundance.

NADA   LOTSA

Crank up the Lotsa!

Spirit is Infinite. Like, In-fin-ite. That's a lot of a lot of a lot! When I'm experiencing not-a-lot in some area of my life, it's a reminder for me to tap into the infinite resources of the Divine. Whether it's money, or friends, or time, Spirit has magical ways of allowing more flow into my life. I just have to make myself available to it. Today I practice allowing the Lotsa!

I am open to Lotsa. I let Spirit bless me with Its riches!

January 12

There are lots of ways to pray. Like everyone, I have my own way of talking to the Source of Creation. Sometimes I have a lot to say. Other times, especially when I'm really hurting, I may only be able to say *Help*. Whatever I say, I know that Spirit is always listening. Spirit loves me unconditionally, whether I'm happy or sad, talkative or not. That's the best part, knowing that *however* I am, I am loved.

I am bathed in the Love of Source. I speak freely.

January 13

One of the best things I can do for myself is learn to approve of myself just as I am. Maybe I'm sad. That's okay. Maybe I'm angry. That's okay too. Maybe I'm so happy I want to burst. That's just as okay as everything else I may be doing or feeling in any moment. The more I learn to approve of myself in every moment, the more loving I become to myself and others. It's like magic!

I approve of myself right here and now. No matter what!

January 14

My dreams were given to me by Spirit. My inspiration and passion are Divine Guidance, pointing me to my greater good. When progress seems slow, I remind myself that a little sprout's final push through the dirt takes more energy than all the rest of its growth. Frustration can be a clue that I'm close. I hang in there and remember the dream!

My dreams came from Spirit. I move in the direction of the Divine's ideas for me.

January 15

I see the perfection of diversity today. I see it in the millions of cells in my body, each expressing in their own way. I see it in the superb variety of plants and animals on this planet. One Source infinitely expressing. So many beautiful beings sharing this floating orb we call Earth. The same, yet each perfectly unique. Life is amazing. *All* of it!

I see the One Source in everything today.

January 16

Is there anything better than a reading break?

Ahhhhhh....

(The answer is NO! Just in case you were wondering...)

Taking a "break" is really not a break at all. When I allow myself time to do something I enjoy, all kinds of things are going on! My body relaxes. Perspective is gained. New ideas are nurtured. Indeed, my productivity actually *increases* when I give myself time and space to step away from busyness. Today I allow this balance. I make time for "breaks" that aren't really breaks at all!

I take "breaks" today. My whole life gets better!

January 17

Everywhere I go, surprises await. Today I open to the wonderful surprises the Universe has in store for me. When I am in joyous expectation of beautiful surprises throughout my day, that is what I draw to me. Today I open to the magic. I open to the wonder. I open to Spirit's love for me. When each wonderful surprise comes, I thank Spirit. My gratitude keeps me open for more. Today I am open.

Spirit, surprise me today!

January 18

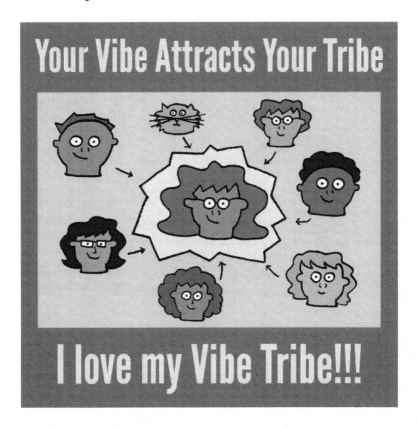

When I surround myself with people who understand me, I feel free and expansive. My Vibe Tribe is an alive, ever-changing entity. It may include tons of folks or just one or two. It can include animals and people who are no longer on this plane. The energy and support I get from my Vibe Tribe allows me to take chances in the world. And I do the same for them! We help each other get better and better every day.

I vibe with my Tribe today. We are unstoppable!

January 19

My mind can be a crowded place. So many different thoughts in there! Then I stop for a minute. Or two. Or thirty. I breathe. I relax. My mind may still be chatty and crowded with thoughts, but this simple practice of stopping and breathing allows some space to come. Like giving the body a massage or a soak in a bath, my mind emerges refreshed and revived. *Ah, the spa!*

I allow my mind time to renew and refresh.

January 20

One of the most effective things I can do to improve my life takes only a minute. When I first wake up, I can visualize my day ahead. I can picture everything going smoothly and easily. I can see myself having fun and enjoying everything I do. I can see myself having harmonious relationships with everyone around me. Then I can get up, go about my day, and watch the magic happen.

I set my intention for a wonderful day. I love my life!

January 21

When I'm in a bad (or crappy) mood, I have a choice. I can allow my mood to wreak havoc, toxifying my inner and outer environment. Or I can feel my feelings, let them run through me, and then reframe the situation – whatever it is – from something that *hurts* me to something that *heals* me. The choice is always mine. Crappy or Happy. Seems easy when you think about it!

Happy is a great choice. Happy here I come!

January 22

Animals are such great teachers. They don't stop themselves from enjoying their lives. When they want to have fun, they go for it! Animals remind me that fun is everywhere – in a piece of string, in a ball, or in simply running around. My life holds endless sources of amusement. The more I look for them, the more I find them.

I remember to play. I skip, I laugh, I enjoy my world!

January 23

It's easy to get distracted by the world around me. Especially when I'm in the process of affirming new good. *Where is it? I don't see it! I don't believe it will ever happen!* When I compare my affirmations with what I see in my present circumstances, I may get discouraged. But when I close my eyes in the process of affirming, I see the truth. My good is already here!

My Good is mine. I see it and I know it!

January 24

When you're not in the mood for smiling, try whipping out a fake smile!

It has many of the same benefits as true smiling, and before you know it, you may be smiling for real.

My smile is like a superpower. It has the capacity to change lives for the better every time it's used. This is true whether I'm smiling for real or busting out a fake smile. Today I practice smiling as much as I can, whether I'm feeling it or not. I smile at friends. I smile at strangers. I smile at myself in the mirror. I let my superpower do its thing, and I allow myself to reap the benefits!

I am a smiling superhero today!

January 25

Keeping score in a relationship never gets me the results I want.

ME	9	8	4	11	5	3	12	8	13	73
YOU	0	0	.3	0	1	0	0	.2	0	1.5

Today I let go of keeping score.
I give love freely & I am filled with joy!

Whenever I start keeping score, I've already lost. Today, I step back from keeping score. Instead, I look for the good in others. What are they doing right? What do they care about? What makes them happy? When I view others from a perspective of love and caring, love and caring permeates my whole world. I feel better about everyone – including myself!

My score-keeping days are over. I'm a joy-keeper now!

January 26

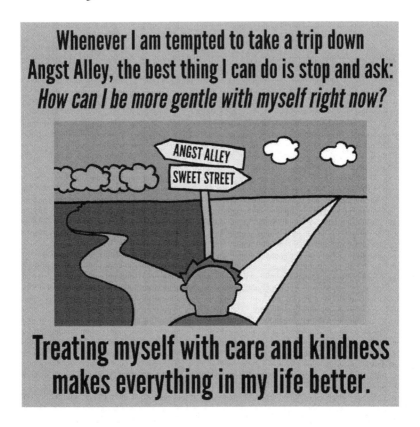

Whenever I am tempted to take a trip down Angst Alley, the best thing I can do is stop and ask: *How can I be more gentle with myself right now?*

Treating myself with care and kindness makes everything in my life better.

If I'm about to go into an internal freak-out about something, I can pause. I can take a breath. This is a powerful moment of choice. Yes, I can traipse down Angst Alley and get my knickers in a serious twist. But there's another way. When I remember to be gentle with myself, my tension eases. My knickers untwist. Gentleness helps to make everything easy and smooth.

When I'm gentle with myself, I walk on Sweet Street.

January 27

The more I realize what a beautiful and powerful person I am, the more I see that my words are an extension of this beauty and power. As such, I choose my words carefully. Whom do I want to uplift today? Whom do I want to encourage? There is so much good to do in the world, and my words are a part of this good. I am grateful to have the opportunity to use language to uplift others – and myself!

My words are powerful. They do good work in the world!

January 28

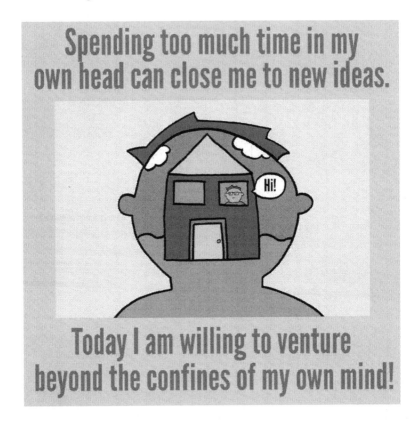

My mind is a wonderful place. I can use it to affirm new good and visualize magical outcomes. But when I spend too much time in my own head without the fresh air of new ideas, things can get a little claustrophobic. That's when it's time to get outside myself and take a little stroll in the big wide world. When I return to the solitude of myself, I am renewed and refreshed.

I am open to discovering new and exciting things!

January 29

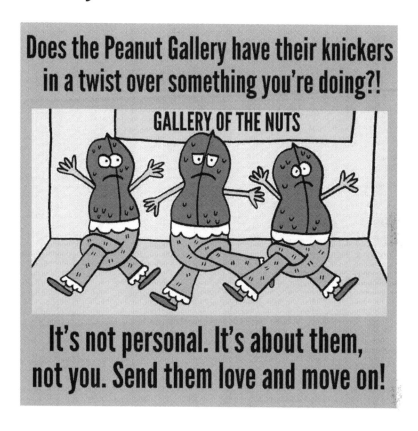

Does the Peanut Gallery have their knickers in a twist over something you're doing?!

GALLERY OF THE NUTS

It's not personal. It's about them, not you. Send them love and move on!

Whenever someone is getting agitated by something I'm doing, or something I *am*, especially when their reaction is out of proportion, I remind myself that it's not about me. It's about them. That doesn't mean I have to be cruel or dismissive. Indeed, it's a sign that a twisted-knickered peanut is in need of some love! I may show this love with my kindness, or just in my thoughts. Either way, it helps.

I send Love to everyone today, even the peanuts!

January 30

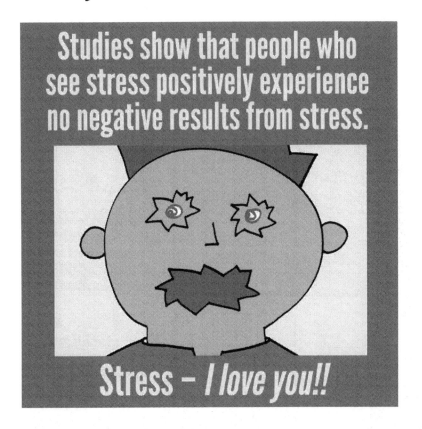

There are many ways to respond to life. Stress is one of them. But when I change my attitude – seeing my life as full and exciting, instead of stressful – then everything changes. Including my old "stress." This doesn't mean I can't include chill time for balance. That's always a good thing. But when my life is super full, I can enjoy it!

I love my full, rich life. Thank you, Spirit!

January 31

I am made of the One Infinite Life that expresses as everything. I am amazing! I can digest food, grow hair, and sing a song all at the same time! I am never the same from one moment to the next. I am ever-changing and evolving. And there is no one else just like me. Never has been. Never will be. I am completely amazing. Today, I'm gonna work it!

I just can't help myself! I know my Awesomeness today.

February 1

When I forget who I am, spending time in nature can help me remember. The Power that made me is the same Power that created nature. The beauty of a flower is my beauty. The strength of a tree is my strength. The flow of a stream is my flow. When I allow myself to connect with the energy of nature, I remember how strong and beautiful I am. And I thank nature for helping me remember.

I love and respect the natural world – and myself!

February 2

The Peace that passeth understanding is never more than a breath away.

I breathe Peace.

Where's the peace? Sometimes it can feel really far away. If I get caught up in drama – and let's face it, there's drama everywhere – it's easy to lose sight of peace. But help is only a breath away. I can close my eyes and inhale. Then exhale. I can breathe slowly and consciously again and again, until I feel the peace that lives in me. What a great place for peace to live – right here inside me.

Peace lives in me. I am grateful!

February 3

Hello! My name is Fred. I'm here to help! If you're ever in a pinch, just let me know. Actually, even if you're **not** in a pinch, you can let me know! I am one of many helpers in the unseen realm who are here to serve you. Humans are funny – they think they need to do everything all by themselves. But you actually make yourself a lot more powerful and effective when you allow yourself to be helped. Give it a try!

I am open to help from seen and unseen sources. I love it!

February 4

There are so many ways to remind myself how amazing I am. I can look to my past. I can see how I've grown and changed. I'm an ever-evolving soul, made up of millions of cells, floating and spinning through space at roughly 1,000 miles per hour. And I could go on! I am made of the Divine stuff of life. I understand that even as I continue to grow, I am a perfect Divine being right now.

Today I remember my Divine Nature.

February 5

What I wear can dictate how I feel. I wear my workout clothes and I feel like an athlete. I wear my favorite pair of pajamas and I feel comforted. And then there's that item of clothing that makes me feel ready to take on anything life throws my way. Whenever I need a boost, I wear *that!* Dynamic clothes remind me of the infinite possibilities of the Divine. *I can do anything!*

I strut my stuff today. Spirit struts with me.

February 6

There are as many different relationships with a Higher Power as there are people on the planet. Today, I strengthen this relationship. My Higher Power is always with me, even when I forget or try to push it away. It loves me unconditionally. As I strengthen our relationship, I strengthen my awareness of love. What a gift!

I am cherished and adored by my Higher Power. I allow myself to feel this Love today.

February 7

There is no one like me. I am a unique creation of the Divine. The more I embrace who I am – *exactly* who I am, *everything* about me – the more I am allowing the Divine to express as me. That's amazing! I am co-creating with an awesome and mighty Force. This Force is helping me bring my unique gifts and talents to the world. What a blessing – to myself and the world!

I am an amazing expression of Spirit!

February 8

I have lots of different voices in my head. Some are really helpful. Others? *Not so much.* My fear voice and my low self-esteem voice are closely related. Ultimately, they're trying to keep me safe, but they do so at the expense of my growth and expansion. I am learning to hear what they have to say, and then totally ignore them. What do they know? *Not very much.* I do much better without them!

I move forward with ease and confidence. I am blessed.

February 9

When I'm feeling disconnected from Life, there's a great way to connect again. The best part is that it's something I do all the time – breathing! When I become conscious of my breath – in and out, in and out – I become more aware of the Life Force that sustains me. I don't have to earn it. I don't have to do anything to deserve it. It's already mine. Right here in each breath.

I breathe Life. I am Life. I celebrate my Life today!

February 10

When I'm feeling stressed, I take a ride in an imaginary hot air balloon.

Wheeeee! My "problems" look a lot smaller from up here!

Stress is no fun! When I'm stressed, I tend to feel overwhelmed. It's hard to see things in their proper perspective. That's when little tricks, like taking a ride in an imaginary hot air balloon, come in handy. Up I go, high above my stressful situation. I'm floating in the clouds, looking down upon all the little people, including me. I see that my problems aren't as big as I think. All is well. *Really!*

I see the bigger picture today. *Whew!*

February 11

I am awesome. It doesn't matter if I believe it. It doesn't matter how I say it. Just uttering these words has the power to change me for the better. After all, the phrase *I am* has creative power. It contains the energy and presence of the Divine *I Am*. So there's that! And then I add *awesome*. As in *impressive, magnificent, awe-inspiring*. Yes – that is what I am! And as I say it, I become it. How awesome is that?!

I am. I am awesome. *I am!*

February 12

It's pretty hard to hate a baby. They're so cute and sweet and innocent. They haven't done anything wrong yet, or hurt anyone's feelings. The Grumpy McGrumpertons in my life were babies once. When I remember this, and send love to that innocent part of them, I strengthen my own soft, innocent self. It feels good to love, and it feels good to see others with love.

I see the softness and sweetness in all life.

February 13

The best gift I could ever get is here with me every day – my life! What a beautiful thing! My life is mine to do with whatever I want. Today I remember that freedom. Are there changes I want to make? Are there things I want to do that I've been putting off? I'm in charge. I get to make choices that are best for me, even if others may not understand. That's okay – they have their own lives to be in charge of!

I'm the boss of me. Today and every day!

February 14

I allow myself to slow down. I allow my thinking to slow down, to find space between my thoughts. As I do this, the space between my thoughts expands. In this opening, I feel the Divine more fully. When I am not identifying with the ego-thinking self, I feel the truth. I am one with the All. I am one with the infinite Self of all life. I am Love itself.

I still myself and allow my mind to follow. I experience the Truth. I am Love.

February 15

A Test to Determine How Spiritual You Are

Pick One

☐ A. I accept myself and others exactly as they are.

☐ B. Accept myself and others?! No way! I'm totally messed up. And so is everyone else.

A. Spiritual Badass: You know that acceptance is the key to serenity and alignment with Truth.

B. Badass in Training: Keep working it! Accept where you are and be open to greater peace.

It's easy to think that if only everyone around me changed, everything would be better. True spiritual maturity is realizing that I am the point of power for change. When I change myself and my attitudes, I realize that everyone around me is doing the best they can. I can practice loving them just as they are. I can also practice loving myself, even when I forget to accept others or myself.

I accept everything today. Even my lack of acceptance!

February 16

I have ideas in my head about what is spiritual and what isn't. Today I let those go! Everything is spiritual! The Life Force that created everything is *in* everything. Therefore, wherever I look, there It is. I bring this awareness to all I do today – including and especially those things I enjoy. My pleasure in beloved activities is one of the many ways Spirit loves me. How wonderful!

I bask in the pleasures of life. Spirit basks with me.

February 17

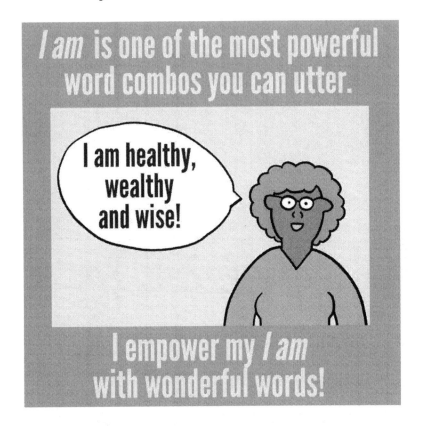

I am whole. I am blessed. I am loved. What wonderful truths to saturate my awareness! It's great to say and think such things when I am feeling these truths. It's also great to say and think such things when I'm feeling out of alignment. After all, they're already true. I *am* whole! I *am* blessed! I *am* loved! Bringing this to my awareness allows me to remember the truth. And celebrate it!

I am whole. I am blessed. I am loved. Yay!

February 18

Have you noticed that you often learn more from failure than from success?

Best
Fail

I love my failures! They help me grow!

Everything is Spirit loving me. If I think I have made a mistake or failed at something, I see that it is Spirit showing me how I need to grow. When I listen and follow these messages, I am following Spirit's lead. I am being inspired to grow in *exactly* the right way for me! This always leads to greater joy, peace, and happiness. Today, I see the perfection of my mistakes and failures.

My mistakes and failures? They are Spirit loving me!

February 19

I have resources inside me that I don't know about. Not until I am faced with a situation where I get to use them. Maybe it's a new job. Maybe it's meeting someone new. Maybe it's changing a behavior or setting a boundary. Whatever it is, I know I can handle it. I call upon my ninja superpowers, fueled by Spirit. After all, with Spirit on my side, I can handle anything!

I am Spirit's ninja. We rock my life!

February 20

Fear is a message from my Higher Self. When I'm afraid, I know it is one of two messages: 1) I need to change course and get out of there fast. 2) I am believing a lie. If the ego self tells me a lie but I *don't believe* it, I feel nothing. But if I tell myself a lie and *believe* it, I feel bad! And terrorizing myself? That's just mean.

I don't terrorize myself. I am nice to me today.

February 21

Today I treat my life like a Facebook news feed...

I make peace with ("Like") everything that comes along!

When I resist events, circumstances, and people, it doesn't feel good. Indeed, it often means that the events, circumstances, and people start to take up more and more space in my head and heart. No fun! Instead, I practice relaxing into the *now*. Into what *is*. There's beauty in everything that exists, just as it is. After all, Spirit created it. And Spirit knows what It's doing!

I look for and celebrate Divine perfection today.

February 22

Time is magical. With it comes wisdom. And humor. And perspective. It's wonderful to allow time to work its magic and gift me with all these things. It's also wonderful to use my imagination and visualize all the gifts that time will bring to my current challenges. The more I look for humor and perspective, the more I find it. Not just in the future, but now.

Wisdom and humor and perspective are mine. Right now!

February 23

It's one thing to feel the calling of my next greater good. This is healthy contrast, pulling me forward into the next expression of my life. However, when I have what I want, and I *still* feel a longing? I check my thinking. Am I just telling myself an old story? I get present and notice all that I have. I allow myself to feel gratitude and joy for this day and all that's in it. The *now* moment is where I find peace.

I am present. I feel the joy of *All That Is* right here.

February 24

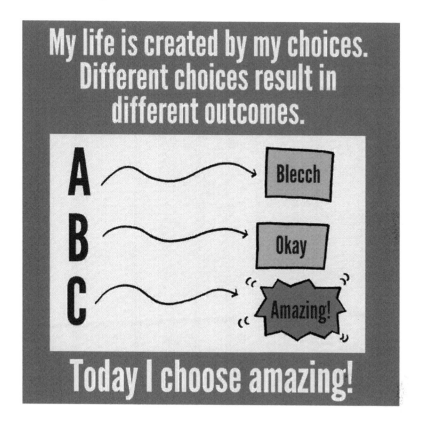

I am always at choice. It may not *feel* like it at times, but choice is always here. In difficult situations that I can't change, I can choose my attitude. In difficult situations that I *can* change, I can choose a different path. Today I look for my choices. When I need help making a choice, I ask for it. When I need Spirit's guidance in making a choice, I ask for it. My choices have the power to create an amazing life.

My choices set me free. I choose wisely today.

February 25

It's easy to think of meditation as a solo pursuit. After all, even if I'm surrounded by other meditators, *I'm* still the one meditating. What's also true is that I am created and sustained by Divine Power, and meditation is a process of connecting with this Power. So why not ask It for help in my meditation?! When I do this, my meditation practice becomes even more connected. How groovy is *that?!*

Spirit helps me in all things – even my meditation!

February 26

Baths and showers aren't only great for hygiene, they're also great for clearing your energy.

I cleanse my mind, body, and spirit!

When I've had a long, hard day, there's nothing more rejuvenating than taking a bath or shower. I can allow the stress and strain to simply pour off me with every drop. I can also take mini baths and showers during the day. When I need a little boost and clearing, I go to a faucet and wash off my face and wrists. This helps clear my energy and leaves me refreshed and renewed.

Water is my friend. I celebrate its cleansing energy today.

February 27

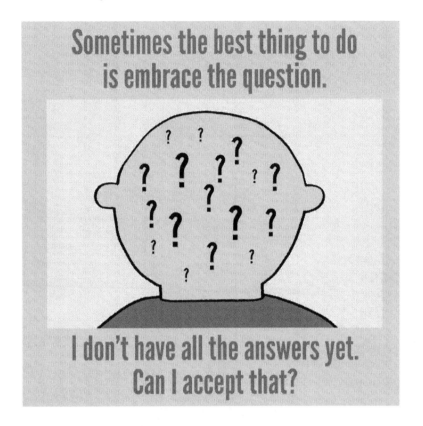

Sometimes the best thing to do is embrace the question.

I don't have all the answers yet. Can I accept that?

When I am in the midst of the unknown, I may cling to answers. Sitting in the big *I Don't Know* can be uncomfortable. But the way to true clarity and wisdom is to rest in the unknown. If I rush too quickly to answers, they won't be the right ones. Instead, I wait. I am patient. I allow Divine Life to guide me. Slowly and surely, all is revealed. I know what I have to do.

I rest in the Unknown. I am at peace.

February 28

On this day, on this glorious Planet Earth, I do hereby accept my Advanced Degree in Awesome. I earned it! Yes, there were days when I didn't yet know the high degree of Awesome that I am. I was deluded into thinking that I wasn't enough. But those days are over. Now I shine! Now I plant my Advanced Degree in Awesome firmly in my heart, mind, and soul. I *am* Awesome. And I know it!

I shine my Awesome all over the place!

February 29

Random Meditation Thought #9587:
If I were young and hip and had a band,
I'd call it Irreplaceable Fish.
That would be cool.

Ommmmmmmmm.

Hello! I'm your mind when you're meditating! Isn't it amazing how many thoughts I can come up with in such a short space of time?! Isn't it weird that **supposedly** you're meditating, but I'm just going on and on about all kinds of stuff?! Like the Irreplaceable Fish band. And how groovy fish are. And how having an aquarium is so relaxing. And.... Oh yeah, sorry. Don't mind me. You're meditating! Ommmmmm.

I watch my thoughts today. What a ride!

March 1

Sometimes I'm hard on myself. There's always so much to improve! But when I get too caught up in all the ways I could be better, I lose sight of how amazing I already am. Today I look for all the things I'm doing well. And there are lots of them! I also take time to appreciate myself for simply being. I am a miracle even when I'm doing nothing at all. I rock – that's all there is to it!

I am an awesome, amazing, incredible being!

March 2

What's going on inside my head? When I start to pay attention to my mind, I notice all kinds of thoughts in there. Some thoughts serve me well. Others are like little pests, undermining my well-being. When I notice a pest, I flip it around. What's the truth behind the pest's lie? Once I uncover the truth, I focus on that. And the best part? Spirit backs me up. Spirit knows my Truth.

Spirit has my back. And my mind!

March 3

Spring cleaning isn't just for houses.
What attitudes can I let go of?
Doubt? Cynicism? Second-guessing?

I let go of attitudes that
no longer serve me!

As I go through life, I am benefitted by clearing out the cob-webs from time to time. This is true in my mental as well as my physical environment. Any effort I put into such a pur-suit is *so* worth it! I love having a clean house. It feels so peaceful and relaxing. I also love having new mental attitudes. As I let go of old constricted beliefs, I feel more present and powerful.

I clear out my environment, inside and out!

March 4

I am intimate with the Infinite!

I am made of Infinite Intelligence. What an incredible thing! The life force that made me is right here. It is closer to me than anything else because it *is* me. I couldn't get any closer to the Infinite than I already am. Becoming more *aware* of this, however, *is* something I can do. Every day, in every way, I can become more and more aware of my coziness with Infinity.

I cozy up to Infinite Intelligence. How sweet!

March 5

When I try to fit into other people's ideas and expectations of me, it can feel like I'm trying to squeeze the sky into a tiny bottle. Same goes for when I'm trying to be like someone else. I am a unique expression of Spirit. The best way to honor that is to simply be myself. This takes courage sometimes, especially when I'm up against those inner or outer expectations of how I *should* be. Today I let those go!

I am free to be the sky. I am fabulous!

March 6

I can fight the flow of my life, but what would be the point? I don't want to spend my life fighting. That's exhausting! When I go with the flow, Spirit is with me. When I go with the flow, I am aligning with vast resources of help and support. When I go with the flow, my life runs *merrily merrily merrily* along. Going with the flow is fun. Going with the flow is freeing. Going with the flow is *me.*

I go with the flow, *merrily I go!*

March 7

There is a saying: *What you want to get is what you most need to give.* When it comes to hugs and love, the perfection is multi-layered. As I give the hugs I long for, I get them back immediately! This is just like everything in life. There is a law of circulation. Today I allow myself to be in the flow of the perfect circulation of love. Today I hug others. As I do so, I am aware that Spirit is hugging me.

I look for what I need and I give it. Starting with hugs!

March 8

There are times in my life when there seems to be no clear path forward. When that happens, the path forward is within. Spirit is letting me know that it's time to take a moment, or two or three, to simply *be*. Inside me is a vast wellspring of wisdom. When my path turns inward, I have the opportunity to connect with this inner richness. Through that connection, the next steps are gradually revealed.

I turn within. My next steps are there.

March 9

You can send love and light to anyone and anything...

I send love and light all over the place!

It's great to be able to help people when they need it. But sometimes that's not possible. They may reject my help. Or I may not have the resources to offer right now. There is one resource I can always offer, however, and that's my love. I can send someone a loving thought. I can imagine them happy and whole. I can see light all around them, enlivening and blessing their lives.

I am a source of Love and Light. I send it out to the world!

March 10

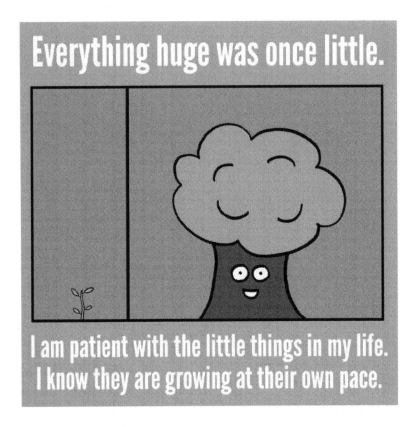

Everything huge was once little.

**I am patient with the little things in my life.
I know they are growing at their own pace.**

I am growing new things in my life all the time. Maybe it's a new project. Maybe it's a new belief. Maybe it's a new way of being in the world. Whatever it is, it deserves my utmost patience. In order to grow to their fullest potential, new things need to be allowed the luxurious process of branching out, little by little. The result? A fully formed, strong and powerful creation. No longer little, but big and mighty.

I nurture what's new. I treat it with tender loving care.

March 11

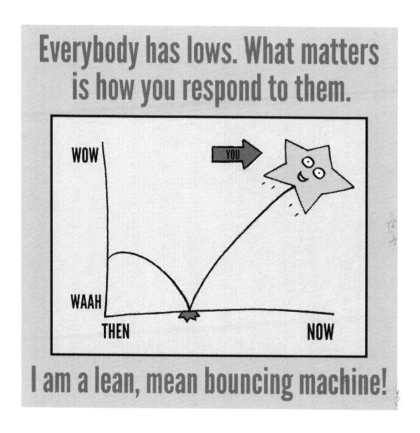

Whatever happens in my life, I am ready. I am always guided and supported by Divine Love. With this support, I am able to see the positive side to everything, even things that others may deem "negative." Sure, I may have feelings of sadness and disappointment. I allow all my feelings to flow through me. Then I pick myself up and get bouncing. I am made stronger and more resilient all the time.

Bouncing is fun. Wheeeeee!

March 12

I allow myself time to chill. I allow myself time to do whatever I want, whether it's reading or gardening or meditating or watching movies or doing nothing at all. I know what makes me feel relaxed and centered, and I take time to do this on a regular basis. If I can take one day a week to chill, I do. If it's only a few hours a week at first, I do that. My chill time makes everything in my life better.

I breathe. I chillax. I am worth it!

March 13

Speak your truth! Sing your song!
Bang your drum!

I live out loud today!

I am made in the image and likeness of the Divine. Confident in this, I let myself shine today! I don't apologize for being me. I don't hold back. Holding back on my self-expression is holding back on Spirit. And that's just *wrong!* I live out loud, being my full-on self. I understand that there will be people who judge me regardless of what I do. So I let myself do what makes me happy. I am *me*. And it's good!

Today I am the most *me* I can be!

March 14

The little kid inside me wants nothing more than to love and be loved.

I give my inner kid lots of love today.

Today, I am aware of my inner child. I love this sweet one within me. I treat them as I would a child in real life: with love, care, and kindness. I am gentle with my inner child. I pamper them in healthy ways. As I love them, they feel safe. As they feel more safe, they come out and play more. As they play, my whole life is more fun. Loving my inner child is healing. I heal myself today.

My inner child is sweet and lovable. I love my kid today!

March 15

I'm the only one who can be inside my mind. If I could hire someone else to meditate for me, I would miss a golden opportunity. Gaining greater awareness of my thoughts, and the emotions they spark, is a life-changing process. The more awareness I gain, the more power I have to create a life that works for me and others. Meditation is a gift that keeps on giving!

I am a fearless investigator of my own mind.

March 16

What do I want to do today? What fun thing could I add to my day? Is there someone I want to include in my little adventure? Or do I want to do it all by myself? Or maybe I want to plan something more elaborate – a trip or a retreat. If there's something fun (or even scary) that I've always wanted to do, I don't let myself put it off any longer. The time is now. Amazing memories, here I come!

I am an Amazing Memory Maker. What fun!

March 17

I am made of Divine stuff. Every cell, every muscle, every tissue, every fiber of my being is made and sustained by Universal Intelligence. In other words, I am a complete and total miracle! *And there's more.* I am not *just* a miraculous physical being. I am also a soul, a vibrant spirit. And boy howdy, what an incredible soul I am! Today I let myself appreciate how amazing I am. Thank you, Spirit!

I bask in my Awesome Sauce existence.

March 18

There are lots of people who may have ideas about what I should be doing. Good for them. It's great to have opinions. Their opinions, however, have *nothing* to do with me! When someone tells me I'm doing something wrong – or who I *am* is wrong – I remember the truth. I remember that who I am and what I do is *my* business. Mine and Spirit's. No one else gets a say in that. How liberating!

I respect myself and my life. I know my Truth!

March 19

There is nothing more powerful than spiritual practice. It allows me to remember who and what I am – a manifestation of the Divine. When I get lost or feel afraid, my spiritual practice gets me back on track. I sit quietly and breathe in Spirit's love. I take a walk in nature. I move my body and center myself in Spirit's power. There are many forms of spiritual practice. I find mine and do them.

I take time for spiritual practice every day. I am full.

March 20

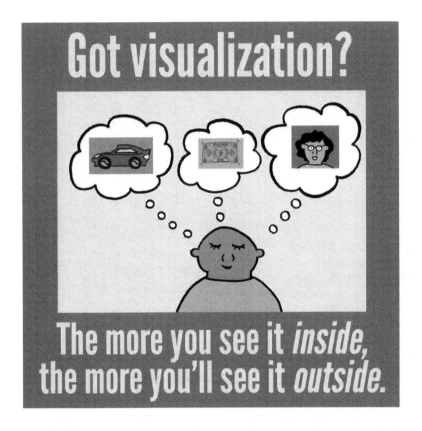

Visualization is one of the most incredible tools I have. I am absolutely free to visualize whatever I want. Wow! That's an *amazing* thing. Today I remember this freedom. What new good do I want to welcome into my life? What does it look like? How am I feeling in the receiving of it? Even just a few minutes of visualization a day can bring incredible results. I play with this power today.

I see it. I feel it. I welcome it!

March 21

I am open to all my feelings. Some feelings are fun to feel. Others are a little more uncomfortable. The most uncomfortable thing, however, is resisting my feelings. When I do that, they get stuck inside me. Then all kinds of shenanigans ensue! I am learning that it's *way* better to simply allow my feelings to flow. *Hello, feeling! What do you have to share? I hear you. Thank you. Bye-bye!*

My feelings flow through me. I listen and release.

March 22

Peace is my birthright.

Peace isn't something I need to earn. I don't need to go to school to get it. I don't need to convince anyone else to give it to me. I don't even need to convince *myself* to give it to me. Peace is already here, inside me. A great way to remember this is by noticing my breath. As I inhale, I feel peace expand inside me. As I exhale, I share my peace with the world. Peace meets peace. I am full.

I breathe peace. I am peace.

March 23

My intuition never fails me. I may fail *it* by not trusting it, and I may need to learn how to listen, but my intuition is always there. The more I commit myself to building a relationship with my inner knowing, the stronger it gets. In big decisions and small ones, I get quiet and listen. Where should I go? What should I do? What should I *not* do? My intuition knows. I trust it today.

I listen to the part of me that knows.

March 24

True wealth?
Knowing your inner worth.

It's the Best. Thing. Ever.

I am a goldmine! My mind is full of infinite ideas and inspirations. My heart is full of love. There are so many lives for me to change for the better, including my own. When I know how powerful I am, I become that much more effective in the world. Today I know my worth. Today I celebrate my Shiny Golden Soul. I sparkle. I glow. I have so much to give!

I am a goldmine of love and inspiration.

March 25

Excuses are like bags of garbage. When you don't dispose of them, they start to stink. Plus they're a pain to carry around. Today, I let go of my stinking excuses. They're heavy and I don't need them anymore. The Divine has an incredible plan for my life. When I follow it, everything gets so much better. Getting rid of my excuses is the best thing I can do!

I am free of excuses today. I follow Spirit's lead.

March 26

One of the best ways to help someone shine their light is to shine yours.

Let your big, bold beautiful light shine!

When I see others shining their light, it inspires me to go for it and shine my own. As I live my life to the fullest, allowing my bright light to be seen, I am an inspiration to others. I allow myself to shine my Truth today. I listen to my inner guidance, and I follow that knowing. I know it is good to do this, for me *and* for the rest of the world!

I shine my light today. It's good for everyone!

March 27

Come by here, Spirit. Opening to Spirit's assistance in prayer, word, or song is a practice of grace. In asking, I am acknowledging that I can't do it alone. In receiving, I am allowing Spirit to expand my life in wonderful ways. The process of gathering with others to pray, sing, and ask for Help amplifies this grace and expansion. The words, the music, the prayer. I allow myself to be uplifted today.

I open to grace today. I let Spirit bless me.

March 28

I am where I am. And sometimes, to get where I want to be, I need to leap from where *I am* to a brand new *I am*! Today I am willing. I am willing to fly into the unknown, remembering that Spirit is always with me. Spirit is with me as I fly, empowering my wings and providing me with a safe landing. And then, when I get to the new *I am*, Spirit is here, showing me the way. Until it's time to leap once again!

My faith gives me wings. I fly with my faith today.

March 29

My body is a blessing. It is a faithful servant. It digests my food. It energizes my body with oxygen. It transports me from place to place. My body is the perfect home for my soul to reside. Today I send my body lots of love. *Thank you, body. I know that sometimes I forget to appreciate you, but today I remember how incredible you are. Thank you for all you do. Thank you for always being there for me. I love you, body!*

I send love to my body today. And every day!

March 30

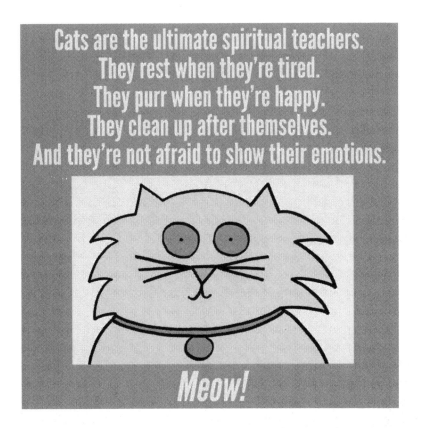

Cats are the ultimate spiritual teachers.
They rest when they're tired.
They purr when they're happy.
They clean up after themselves.
And they're not afraid to show their emotions.

Meow!

I take my cue from cats today. I pay close attention to my inner guidance. I say *No* when I mean *No* and *Yes* when I mean *Yes*. If anyone takes my self-care needs personally, that's on them. I don't need to apologize for my needs. *Cats don't!* It's appropriate to love myself and I know it. Because of this, I purr more. I lounge. I play. I pounce. What a great way to live!

I honor myself with honesty and exquisite self-care.

March 31

Affirmations are an amazing way to let in good. But sometimes affirmations can feel like too big of a stretch. Even an affirmation I've believed in the past. When that happens, I can add willingness to the equation. *I am willing to believe....* Or, if I can't get there, *I am willing to be willing...* My willingness makes me open to new energy, new beliefs, new confidence. My willingness makes me willing!

I am willing to be willing. Miracles await!

April 1

It's April Fools' Day! Today I play the fool in the best sense of the word. I don't know everything, and today I embrace that fact. When I open myself to all that I don't yet know, the Universe rushes in with wonderful, magical surprises. There is so much to learn. There is so much to love. Hit me up, Universe! I'm ready. I'm open. I'm willing.

I am a fool for Love. I let Love surprise me today!

April 2

No one is more spiritual than me. And I am no more spiritual than anyone. We're *all* made of God stuff. So how could anyone be any more spiritual than anyone else? Some folks lose touch with their spiritual sides, but the best thing I can do for them is to love them. Actually, the best thing I can do for *anyone* is to love them, even those who think they're more spiritual than I am!

I am a spiritual rock star. And so is everyone else!

April 3

The Universe is all over me! There is no where I can go – in thought, or word, or deed – that the Universe is not 100% there. This is such great news! I am truly never alone. I am truly supported in everything I do. When I mess up, the Universe is there. When I triumph, the Universe is there. As I open up to this reality more and more every day, I am less and less afraid.

I am held. I am loved. *Always.*

April 4

I have come through many things in my life. When I look at how far I've come, I feel fantastic. When I look at someone else, superimpose their life onto mine, and compare what appears to be the *vastly superior outcome* of their life, I feel like crap. No wonder! I've made up something in my head that has nothing to do with either me or them. Today I let go of the comparison game.

I have come so far! I appreciate this today.

April 5

Getting specific about what I want works well sometimes. Other times, my specificity gets me stuck in a hole of frustration. When that happens, I remember to take a step back. How do I want to *feel* when I have what I desire? Activating the *feeling* allows Spirit to get into motion, bringing me results that may be surprising, unexpected and – most importantly – even better than I imagined!

I *feel* my way into awesome results. Thank you, Spirit!

April 6

Everything responds better when we treat it lovingly – even computers!

I send love to everything!

There is nothing in my life that won't be better off if I send it a blast of love. This includes those things I think of as inanimate objects. Computers, cars, appliances. All of these are made of Divine Substance. As such, they respond well to love from another entity made of Divine Substance – me! As love flows from me to them, I feel a hum of gratitude in response. Everything flows better with love.

I blast Love to everything I see!

April 7

Everything about my life is a miracle. The intricate system of my body. The people who have come into my life at exactly the right time and place. The people who have *left* my life at exactly the right time and place. How much I've grown. How Spirit has supported me. Today I remember the miracles that make up my life. There are so many of them. I give thanks for what has been – and all that is to come!

My life is a miracle. I give thanks!

April 8

When hate is in my face, it can appear to be a mighty force. But it's not. Hate is nowhere near as strong as Love. The momentum of hate always destroys itself. Love, on the other hand, builds and builds. It can't be stopped. There is nothing Love can't fix and no problem it can't solve. Today I see hate for the tiny little annoyance that it is. I celebrate Love's inevitable victory. *Go Love!*

I am on the winning team. The Love Team!

April 9

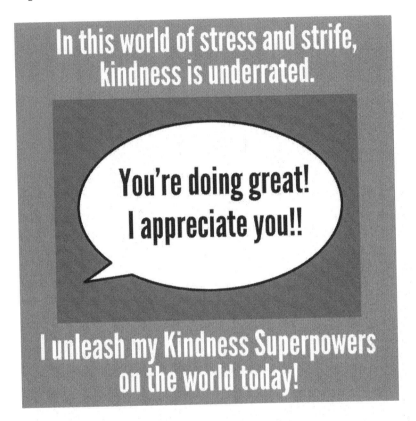

Every moment is a new opportunity for kindness. I can be gentle with someone who is going through a hard time. I can be gentle with *myself* when I need it. I can give an anonymous gift. I can pick up a piece of stray trash. My kindness superpowers are mighty! As I activate them, my whole being is lifted. Who knew I could be so kind and so powerful? *Spirit did!*

Kindness is my religion. I am born again!

April 10

When I need a little pick-me-up, I smile like I'm Mona Lisa.

It reminds me that life is a mystery and wonderful surprises await!

There are lots of ways to bust out my Mona Lisa smile. I can smile gently when I'm meditating. I can Mona Lisa my way down the street, uplifting everyone I see. I can look at myself in the mirror and allow Mona Lisa to spark my imagination. My life is a mystery, even to me. There are so many things I have yet to understand. I go forth in eager anticipation. Mona Lisa leads the way!

I bask in the Mystery. Thank you, Mona Lisa!

April 11

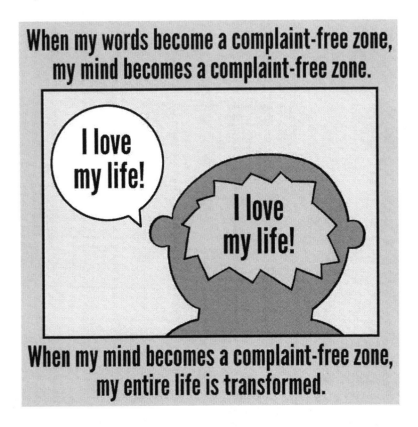

My words are one of my most powerful creations. As such, I treat them with great care. I look for the positive aspects in every situation and release the need to complain. This practice allows me to use the power of language in the best possible way. As my words become more and more positive, so does my mind. As my mind becomes more positive, so does my life. It all starts with my mouth!

I watch my words. And I watch my life blossom.

April 12

Hello there! Our names are Fanny and Rxdrsyydowelly. We are here to wish you a fabulous day! Where we're from, Planet Trigh7f4, we have a tradition. Every morning, we fly to the house of someone we don't know and send them some positive vibes. Today, we picked you! We will be with you all day, backing up everything you do with our exuberant flying monkey juju. If you'd like, we'll stick around every day. After all, we're magical like that!

I allow help in all forms – including magical ones!

April 13

Today I remain steadfast. I stay true to my dreams and move ever closer to them with my choices, my thinking, and my actions. If I'm discouraged, I know that this can be part of the process. I allow myself a short amount of time to have my feelings, and then I turn and get back on course. The only time I fail is when I give up. So I don't give up!

I am unstoppable. I keep on keeping on!

April 14

I am at choice in every moment. What are my choices today? Am I grateful for all I have? Am I grateful for who I am and how far I've come? If not, I get my gratitude on today! I start with things I can genuinely feel grateful for. Then I move on to things that don't usually spark gratitude in me. What do I appreciate about those things? How are they helping me grow? Next thing I know, I'm feeling grateful for *everything*.

I am grateful for my life. *All* of my life!

April 15

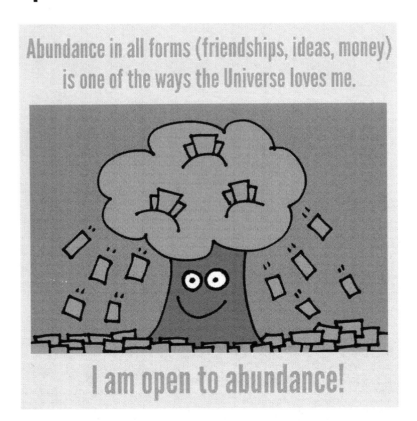

Abundance in all forms (friendships, ideas, money) is one of the ways the Universe loves me.

I am open to abundance!

Every day, in every way, I am prospered. If I forget this, all I have to do is look around. I savor the Flagrant Displays of Awesome of the plants and trees of this planet. I appreciate the never-ending supply of air that invigorates my lungs and body. I delight in the infinite store of ideas and inspirations that live between my ears. The more I bask in abundance around and within, the more it flows to me.

I am an Active and Awesome Abundance Attractor!

April 16

Can you imagine if flowers were afraid to shine for fear of outshining the other flowers?!

Take a tip from the flowers: No one else is diminished by your magnificence. Shine on!

When I look at a bed of flowers, I see a chorus of colorful creation. Every single member of the chorus is shining. They're not worried about offending the flowers around them. They're *all* beautiful. Indeed, the beauty of each flower combines to make an even greater, beautiful whole. That's what happens when I shine. I help to create an even more beautiful world.

I let my beauty out today. I'm making the world better!

April 17

From the time I was a baby, I have tripped and fallen. And then I've gotten up. When I was little, getting up was simply what I did. Today, I remember that resilience. Falling is simply a part of moving forward. It happens, and it's no big deal! I pick myself up and I try again. I learn from my mistakes. I am grateful for the process. I am grateful for my gracefulness – even as I fall.

I fall down. I get up. I am graceful all the way!

April 18

I am my own best source of advice. Especially when I'm connected to *the* Source. As I tap into Infinite Wisdom within me, I am able to find information that is tailored *just for me*. Imagine that! This is not to say I can't get great ideas from others. Sometimes the Divine speaks through other people. But when I am confused by outside sources of information, I turn within. The answer is always there.

Source is my source. I listen within.

April 19

When I see something clearly with my inner eye, it doesn't matter what I see outside. My inner clarity allows me to move through external circumstances with ease and resolve. In those areas where I do not yet have inner clarity, I can strengthen it with Spirit's help. I can meditate. I can pray. I can visualize. I can ask for Help. Clarity comes and my way is made easy. I am grateful.

Spirit has high expectations for my life. So do I!

April 20

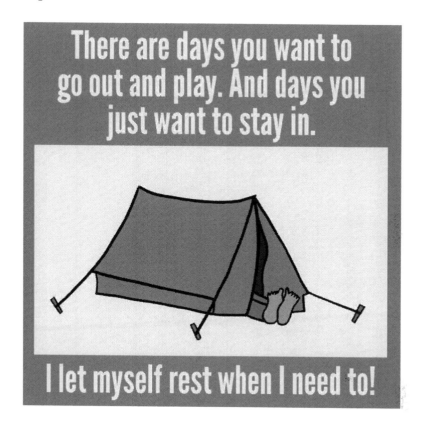

There are days you want to go out and play. And days you just want to stay in.

I let myself rest when I need to!

Sometimes I feel like kicking some major butt! Other times, what I really need is chillin'. Resting is an accomplishment. When I allow myself the rest I need, I am achieving the goal of living a balanced life. With this in mind, I let myself rest deeply, conflict-free. I get all the goodies from my rest. I know that by doing this, I will be all the more ready to kick butt once again!

I live a life of balance today.

April 21

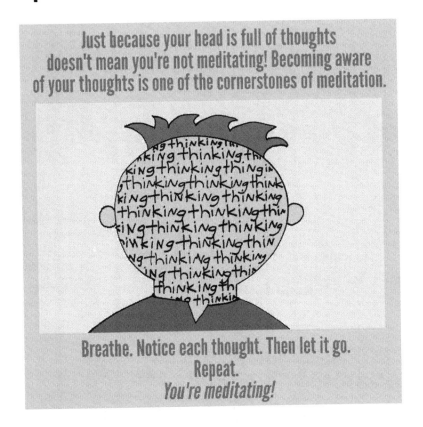

Just because your head is full of thoughts doesn't mean you're not meditating! Becoming aware of your thoughts is one of the cornerstones of meditation.

Breathe. Notice each thought. Then let it go.
Repeat.
You're meditating!

My mind is a chatty thing. Indeed, meditation shows me just how chatty it is. Meditation *also* helps me to create a little space around my chatty mind. The more I can sit and simply listen to the chatter, the more I can begin to step back from it. Little by little, space and peace grow in my mind. Even on those days when all I seem to do is listen to the chatter, I am making a way for peace.

As I listen to the chatter, Peace grows within me.

April 22

I take a moment to appreciate this planet: her earth, her air, her water.

I love my home!

I live in an amazing place. Planet Earth is a vast, beautiful wonder. She has canyons and forests and oceans. She has rivers and valleys and mountains. And then there's the little corner of the planet where I live. Today I give thanks. I give thanks for the vast wonder, and I give thanks for my little corner. I appreciate the beauty of big and small, and I commit to caring for my beautiful home.

I appreciate the beauty of Planet Home.

April 23

I am never alone. But sometimes I feel like I am. In those moments, I may need to wander in isolation for a while before I remember to ask for Help. But Help is always there. There is nowhere I can go that the Divine is not with me. No matter how lonely I become, Spirit never leaves me. I can bring my fear and isolation to the Divine, and It loves me right where I am. Before I know it, I feel whole again.

I am never alone. I am held by Divine Love.

April 24

Fear expresses itself as many emotions – anger, envy, worry. When I recognize fear today, I turn my attention back to Love. I ask myself, *What would Love do?* I am Love. So I allow the answer to come from the depth of my being. I allow Love to guide my words and actions. This includes the practice of loving *me*. When I've discover I've been off the Love track, I get back on. I let Love win, always!

I practice being Love today, in all I say and do.

April 25

Old-school God was a fickle old man who lived in the sky. He loved me one minute and smited me the next.

I love you!

I smite you!

Today I send Old-School God to play shuffleboard with his friends. I trade him in for a wise and loving Higher Power instead.

There are many images of God. Old-School God is one of them. Old-School God is quite a character. He can be loving at times, but then He goes off his meds and smites everyone in sight. Today I let Old-School God go. Today I build my own relationship with my Higher Power. Today I am unconditionally loved, and I know it. What a relief!

I love my God. And my God loves me!

April 26

I am whole and complete. I pursue my passions, and I fill my days with people and activities I love. The more I focus on cultivating love within and around me, the more love comes into my life. In such an atmosphere of love, it's only natural that I draw to me those I call soul mates. Soul mates can be friends or family or sweethearts. Today I celebrate all my soul mates. I give thanks for love.

I love Love. And Love loves me!

April 27

I am a ninja! I am capable of so much more than I know. When I am feeling afraid, I can take a breath, rise above, and do what I need to do. When I am angry, I can take another breath, clear my mind, and calm my soul. I can stick to my beliefs and values, and I can be honest and trustworthy in my interactions with others. I can help others in need. I am not afraid to be a ninja!

I bust out my ninja powers today. I am mighty!

April 28

If I'm feeling bad about myself, I am believing a lie. My inner gremlins are not speakers of Truth. The Truth feels good. I am awesome! So if I don't feel good, I am probably listening to, and agreeing with, my inner gremlins. Today I turn my attention to the Truth. I let the truth sing out through me, drowning out the voices of the gremlins. I feel good. I let the Truth set me free. I rock! *Yay me!*

I let the Truth sing louder than lies today. Cuz I rock!

April 29

Everything amazing started as an idea.

**Nurture your ideas.
Let them become amazing things!**

I have a storehouse of wonderful ideas inside me. Today I focus on them. Which ideas want my attention? Which ideas want to move from the unmanifest realm into the realm of creation? There is nothing more miraculous than an idea moving from thought to form. I can birth this miraculous event by taking my ideas seriously, and doing my part in the wonder of creation.

I nurture my ideas today. I let them shine!

April 30

Everyone needs love and self-care. I am no different than anyone else in this respect. If I think I can push myself too hard and still have anything left to give to myself or others, I am wrong. Today I remember the incredible rejuvenating power of self-care. When I take good care of myself, everyone is the better for it. Including and especially me!

I take impeccable care of myself. Everyone benefits from my self-care!

May 1

Good is contagious. The more good I let into my life, the more I open the channels for good to flow into *every* area of my life. If there is an area where I want more good, today I simply focus on all the good I already have. I don't need to effort. I don't need to force my good to me. It's already here. All I have to do is let it flow. Focusing on my current good is the best way to open the floodgates.

Oodles of Good are already mine. Thank You, Spirit!

May 2

When learning something new, it's great to have help.

I am open to help today.

I can't do everything alone. And thank God for that! Opening myself up to help allows me to grow. It allows me to connect more deeply with others. It allows others to share their gifts with me. When I receive help from others, I am letting Spirit love me. And as I let in this help, learning and growing, I have more to offer others in the future. The cycle of help is a cycle of love. I am part of that cycle today.

I ask for help today. I am part of the cycle of Love.

May 3

Relationships grow and change all the time. Sometimes my relationships grow in ways that make everyone better. And sometimes relationships end up in a place of stagnation. When this happens, it's time to take inventory. Would I be better served by moving on? When I make a choice to leave a relationship because it serves my higher good, I can trust that the higher good of the others involved is served as well.

I release what no longer serves me. I set us all free!

May 4

There is no one else on the earth just like me. Never has been. Never will be. This is a factual reality. I will never happen again! Given the undeniable fact of my absolute uniqueness, I may as well relax into the me that I am. Today I allow myself to follow my passions and grow in the ways only I can grow. More and more each day, I am becoming the me I was meant to be.

I celebrate myself today. I am one of a kind. Yay *me*!

May 5

How I say something is as important as *what* I say. If I find myself affirming a new good, but I notice that I'm speaking with all the forcefulness of a wet noodle, I know it's time to add some *oomph* to the equation. Even if I don't really feel it at first, I can speak *as if* I am the most enthusiastic version of myself. As my mouth and body emulate passion and excitement, my mind follows. The result? My good is mine.

I affirm my Good with confidence and enthusiasm!

May 6

We all have that favorite program we're embarrassed to admit we watch.

The Secret Lives of Portuguese Lesbian Chefs

Go ahead, indulge yourself!

Everyone has guilty pleasures, myself included. Today I take out the *guilty*! I love what I love, even if no one else understands. The books, TV shows, movies, and other pastimes I enjoy are simply that. *Things I enjoy*. Today I claim my joy! No one else has to understand. Only me. Nurturing myself with activities that bring me pleasure is an awesome way to let Spirit love me.

No more guilty for me! I enjoy my pleasures today!

May 7

You can't move forward when your knickers are in a twist.

(Plus it makes it really hard to get dressed in the morning.)

Untie the knot and move on!

When I'm all tied up in knots about something, nothing makes sense. I can't see clearly. I can't act decisively. My mind is muddled with anger, doubt, and fear. Having my knickers in a twist is a part of life – it happens to me just like it happens to everyone. The trick is to catch myself in twisted-knicker mode and make the decision to untie myself. I breathe. I ask Spirit for Help. I free the knot!

I free my knickers today. I untwist and shout!

May 8

I have a wonderful mouth and mind. Together, they make a mighty combination. But sometimes the best use of my mind and mouth is to elect silence. Perhaps there is a truth that I know someone is not ready to hear. Perhaps there is an emotion – in me or someone else – that needs to be simply felt, not talked about. Today I embrace the beautiful spaciousness of Divine silence.

I know when to speak. And when not to.

May 9

Life is full of unknowns. Instead of being afraid of this, I sink into what I *do* know. I am made of Spirit. My entire life is made of Spirit, expressing as Spirit. Life calls me to greater and greater expressions of Spirit. In the face of today's uncertainties, I remember that this is what's happening: Spirit is expressing as me. I surrender the details to The One in charge. As I surrender, I become a master of peace.

Today I release the need to know. I surrender. Ah…Peace.

May 10

I've had a full life. I've had challenging days. I've had cele-bratory days. I've had days that are a wild and wacky combination of the two. And then there's today. However I'm feeling today, I know that I can ride through the feelings, surrender to another sunset, and awaken tomorrow morning, ready for a new day. I take my life a day at a time, a minute at a time. I am ready for each moment.

I am ready for my life. I rise and shine today!

May 11

**Annoying Reminder #456a:
Those who bother you the most
are the most like you.**

(You're welcome. Just doing my job.)

Some people are really good at annoying me. Actually, even though it *seems* like they're the ones who are doing the annoying, the annoyance is really in my mind. I'm choosing to focus on aspects of them I find irritating. Today, I turn my focus within. My laser-sharp critique of others is an indication that there's something in me that needs love and acceptance. I give myself this love today.

I love myself just as I am. I free myself and others!

May 12

When our minds are closed to new things, we can't grow.

I open my mind & let life amaze me!

When I close my mind, everything gets really stuffy. I turn further and further inside myself, where the fresh air of new ideas and inspirations can't find me. Today I remember to keep the door open! I allow the gentle breeze of Spirit's love and illumination to fill my mind and heart. The open flow of ideas invigorates my life. New opportunities and adventures are in store!

As I open my mind and heart, my life is made new.

May 13

When I practice seeing everyone with the eyes of love, a wellspring of love is opened up in me. The more I practice, the easier it gets. I may choose to start with those that are easy to love. Then I can move to those that are more challenging. The more I work it, the more love flows – from me to them, from them to me, and from me to me. Cultivating the flow of love is a beautiful thing.

I see everyone with Love. We are in the Flow!

May 14

Feeling rushed? Stop for a minute and take a deep breath.

Remember: Time is your friend. *You got this!*

Time is a funny thing. Sometimes an hour takes forever. Other times it's gone in a flash. Whenever I'm feeling crunched for time, I remember its flexible nature. Knowing this, I can call upon time's flexibility to work in my favor. As I slow down and take a breath, I feel time expand around me. I feel a sense of spaciousness growing and increasing. Time works in my favor. Every time!

There is plenty of time for everything I need to do.

May 15

How I do something is even more important than *what* I do. If I say something nice, but I do so in a rushed manner, the impact of my kindness is lessened. If I fight for peace, but I do so in a way that is full of strife, my fighting creates more strife and less peace. Instead, I start by finding peace inside me. Everything I do after that is simply perpetuating the peace that I am.

I am Peace. And I share my Peace with the world.

May 16

Meditation allows me to personally get to know my own mind and Spirit. As I practice the art of being present, I notice there is a presence around and through everything. This presence is The All. It is everywhere. It is All That Is. This is what I am. It is where I dwell. I am at home in the midst of the Infinite. Present in the Presence . . . this is my residence, my true address.

I practice the art of presence today. I am where I Am.

May 17

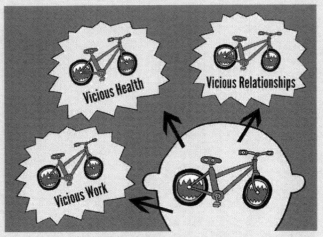

The most vicious part of a vicious cycle is your belief in it, attracting outside events to match.

Vicious Health

Vicious Relationships

Vicious Work

I stop my vicious cycles where they begin – in my mind!

The only place a vicious cycle has any power is in my mind. This is great news! I'm in charge of my mind, so I can stop a vicious cycle in its tracks. Sometimes, if I'm not paying attention, a cycle may get some traction before I notice it. Indeed, sometimes the outside appearance of a "vicious cycle" is what gets my attention. That's okay. It's never too late to turn within and stop the cycle.

I'm in charge of my mind. *Bye-bye, vicious cycle!*

May 18

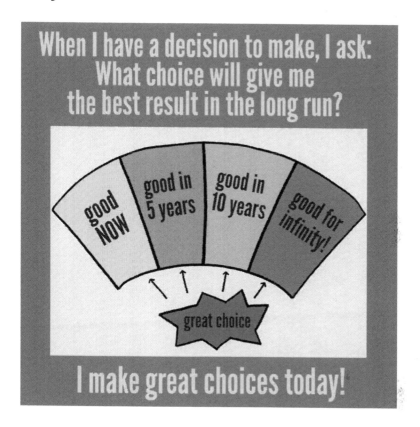

When I have a decision to make, I ask:
What choice will give me
the best result in the long run?

good NOW | good in 5 years | good in 10 years | good for infinity!

great choice

I make great choices today!

Every day, I have choices to make. When I think about what will benefit me the most in the long run, my choices get easier. Expanding my vision to a longer view helps me see the power of my choices. Though today may be only one step in a particular direction, my expanded view allows me to see *all* the good that comes when I walk in that direction. I embrace this longer view today.

I choose wisely today. I step into my greater Good!

May 19

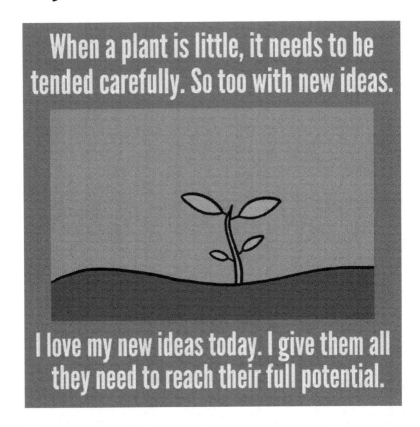

When a plant is little, it needs to be tended carefully. So too with new ideas.

I love my new ideas today. I give them all they need to reach their full potential.

When I see a little plant or animal, my heart opens. It's as if the tenderness needed to care for it is naturally evoked in its presence. Today I remember that the same is true for me and my tender new ideas. They need my love and care. They need to be protected. When I give them this, I am insuring that they will grow up to be strong and healthy. Plus it feels good to care for and nurture myself.

I nurture my tiny ideas into magnificent creations!

May 20

Vision boards are an awesome way to coax your Good to you.

ABUNDANCE!
HEALTH!
LOVE!

I coax wonderful surprises into my life!

The more clearly I can see my good now, as if it is right here, the more powerfully I am drawing it to me. I use empowering tools to support myself in seeing this good. I allow myself to imagine I am in my greater future good right now. When I see it in front of me, in pictures, it supports me in imagining that it's all around me. It is here *now*!

I see my future clearly. My future Good is already here.

May 21

I love letting Spirit lead. Except when I start to doubt. That's when I come up with my own plans, going against Spirit's vision. I'm human, so it's only natural that I go out on my own from time to time. My little excursions are great teaching tools. I get to see what happens when I doubt the Divine! When I've had enough, I pick myself up and let Spirit back in. Everything gets easier after that.

I let Sprit lead. I am safe.

May 22

I am a bright, shiny soul. This is the truth of me, whether I know it or not. Some days I really feel it. Other days I feel a little cloudy. Today? Today I remind myself how frickin' shiny I am! That's how Spirit made me. In Its image and likeness. Powerful. Creative. Full of wisdom and grace. I have so much to offer. I am a beautiful manifestation of the Divine. The Divine is my shine!

This shiny light of mine, I'm gonna let it shine!

May 23

Gratitude is like a healthy plant. It grows and grows and grows! When I find things to be grateful for, including and especially things I might otherwise overlook, my gratitude gets that much stronger. What are the things in my life I might forget to be grateful for? Today I put a spotlight on them. I make a game to find as many things to be grateful for as I can. And then, like a healthy plant, I thrive.

My life is full of things to be grateful for!

May 24

A lot of money is flowing to me now!

OVERFLOWING ABUNDANCE
CASH FLOW
YAY! YAY!
$
BIG BUCKS

I welcome it, and I use it for my good and the good of others!

A lot of money *is* flowing to me now! My job, if I choose to accept it, is to *allow* this money to flow to me. Today I do all I can to strengthen my allowing muscles. I practice gratitude for what I have. I meditate and relax into the abundance that is already mine. I fill my mind with thoughts of plenty and flow. As I do so, I notice richness all around me. And as I notice the richness?! More comes!

A *lot* of money is flowing to me now. I *love* it!

May 25

No matter what is going on in my life, I am safe. No matter whom I am with, or where I am going, I am safe. Today I remember this. Eternally intertwined with this safety is the love of the Divine. I am always held and protected by Divine Love. Even when I feel like I have wandered far away from the loving safety of the Divine, it is always with me.

I am always safe. I am always loved. Always!

May 26

Every time we ask Spirit for help, we get it.

Help!

The trick? Be open to Help in expected and *unexpected* ways.

I know that Spirit always hears me. I also know that Spirit always answers my call for help. Even when I don't get the answer I want or expect, I understand that Spirit's got my back. Sometimes what I *think* is best for me isn't. So today I ask for help, *and* I remain open to the answer that comes, regardless of what the answer might look like.

I ask for help today. I am open to any answer!

May 27

It's easy to love others from afar. But when they get up close? That's when I can see *everything* about them, including aspects that might annoy me. *Just a little.* Those who are close to me also know everything about *me*, which gives *them* the wonderful opportunity to be annoyed as well. Today I embrace my up-close-and-personal peeps for the spiritual practice that they are. We are blessing each other!

I see my up-close-and-personal peeps with Love.

May 28

A benefit of slow progress is it gives me the opportunity to enjoy every step of the way.

Today I bask in each step.

Sometimes things aren't happening as quickly as I think they should. But they're happening at the perfect pace, whether I know it or not. Whenever I get frustrated that things are happening too "slowly," this is a perfect reminder for me to take a breath and notice the beauty of every detail of the journey. There are all kinds of wonderful, beautiful things right in front of me, if I only stop to notice.

I stop. I breathe. I appreciate the beauty of my world.

May 29

My mind is an expert at distortion. It can turn my perfectly normal face into something out of a Picasso painting.

I release my distorted view of myself. I embrace my true beauty!

My mind can be a trickster at times. It convinces me that everything is horrible when it's not. If I'm feeling crappy, this is often a sign that my trickster mind is at it again. Today I look for the signs. Am I seeing something through an all-or-nothing lens? Am I blowing up minor problems and ignoring major blessings? When I find the signs of trick-sterism, I give thanks. I release them and move on.

I'm not fooled by tricks today!

May 30

Some things are easy to learn. Others take a bit longer. In some areas of my life, I have to get sick and tired of being sick and tired before I can ask for Help. That's okay. The important part is to remember to let Spirit in. It's never too late. Spirit is always here, unconditionally loving me. Spirit is always available to pull me out of the sick-and-tireds. Letting go and letting God is amazing!

I let go. I let God. Everything changes for the better.

May 31

The phrase *even better than I can imagine* is magical. By adding it to my repertoire, I am allowing Spirit to blast open any limited visions I may be carting around. Spirit's vision for my good is *always* bigger than mine. When I affirm that I am opening to good that's *even better than I can imagine,* I am giving Spirit permission to surprise and amaze me.

I am opening to a Good that's even better than I can imagine!

June 1

When I tap into the love of Spirit, I understand what peace is. There is nothing more peaceful than knowing that Spirit's love for me is vast and never-ending. I can never stray so far that I am apart from this love. By the same token, when I tap into the peace of Spirit, I know what love is. The beautiful expanse of Spirit's peace belongs to me. I am safe and loved in this peace.

Spirit loves me. I am at peace.

June 2

There's *always* cool stuff going on. When I take a moment to slow down, I notice it. Today I take time to notice. I watch. I listen. I feel. What does the Divine want to show me? I allow myself the space for Spirit to bring me little gifts. The conversation of birds. The splendor of the sky. The touch of air on my skin. The gifts were already here, waiting.

I notice cool stuff today. Thank you, Spirit!

June 3

Hee hee hee. That's funny! *Hee hee hee.* Giggling is good for me. If I'm not getting enough giggles, today I find a way to get some. My sense of humor is unique to me, so I know best what will make me laugh. *Hee hee hee.* If I can make someone else giggle, so much the better! Then there are *two* more gigglers in the world. When the whole world giggles, the planet giggles. And the world is a happier place!

Hee hee hee. **I get my giggles on today!**

June 4

We've gathered here today because you forgot something. You forgot how powerful you are.

Go get 'em! We believe in you!

*Hello! We are a group of specially chosen people. We are everybody who has ever encouraged you. Perhaps you knew us in person. Perhaps we never met, but our presence made you feel inspired. Perhaps we have passed over, but are still in your heart. Here we are, to remind you of your amazingness. If you forgot, **we** didn't! When you forget, **we** don't! Whenever you need reminding, here we are. Inside your heart, mind, and soul. We love you!*

I relish the encouragement of my peeps today.

June 5

Knowing which path to take can be challenging.

The Most Challenging Thing You Will Ever Do in Your Life

I listen to my intuition.
I let it guide my way.

My intuition is my connection with the Divine. My intuition offers me fine-tuned, personalized, highly specific information. Learning to access my intuition is totally worth it! It may take time to learn how to hear it, but the more I practice, the better I get. Today I honor the part of me that knows. Today I give thanks for all the guidance I have received so far, and all that is to come. Today I listen.

My intuition is always with me. I am listening.

June 6

If I am feeling bad, I am believing a lie. This is true whether I am feeling bad about myself or someone else. When I'm feeling bad, not only are my inner squirrels chattering away, but I am listening and agreeing with them. Today I choose to be awake and aware of whom I listen to. Today I listen to the part of me that tells the Truth about myself and others.

I tell myself the Truth. How wonderful is *that?!*

June 7

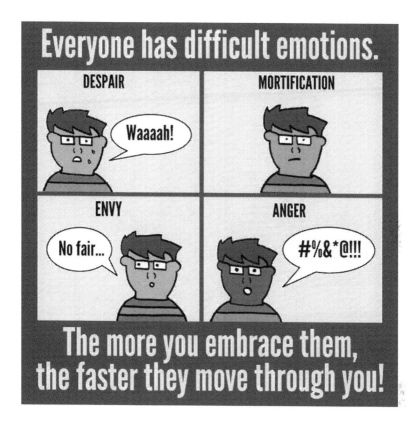

I am aware of my emotions today. What are they trying to tell me? Today I listen. If I am sad, I let myself be sad. If I am happy, I let myself be happy. There are so many emotions to feel. When I simply let them move through me, that's what they do. Move *through* me. This goes for difficult as well as pleasant emotions. As I let them flow, I am at peace.

I feel all my feelings today. I let them flow.

June 8

We all make up stories. All the time. Are your stories serving you?

If so, keep 'em. If not, rewrite them!

I am the most powerful storyteller in my world. When I realize this, my power increases. Now I can *choose* what kind of stories I want to tell. Today I tell stories that serve my life. If I catch myself reciting old stories that make me feel bad, I stop. I close the book on those old stories and start new ones. What power I have! What a great storyteller I am! Today I use my powers for good.

I tell wonderful stories today. My life is better for it!

June 9

My experience is made up of my beliefs. Beliefs are the filter through which I see my world. Today, I tell myself that I am lucky. Indeed, I am downright blessed by angels. Why? Because the Universe adores me. So much so, I am supported with magical fabulousness in every area of life. Cuz I say so! As I come to believe this, it's true. Like magic!

Today I practice the art of believing what I want to.

June 10

Ever feel like doing damage to yourself or others?
Remember the pause that always refreshes.

Meditation: It's cheaper than therapy.
And no one gets hurt.

Anger and agitation have a way of bringing out the worst in me. When I find my thoughts and emotions getting heated, I take a break. I may sit with my eyes closed. I may walk slowly and consciously. Whatever form of meditation I need to do, I do it. As I calm my mind and body, I come back to center. From this more grounded, centered place, I know what to do. *Or not do.* And I am grateful.

I pause. I breathe. I am grateful.

June 11

Keeping score in relationships never makes me a winner. If I'm noticing all the ways I'm better than someone else, or all the ways I'm sacrificing more than someone else, I've become contracted. Today, I focus on giving. I send love to everyone I see. I send love to everyone I think about. I am kind. I am generous. As I open to giving, I step off the scorecard and into the Land of Love.

The more I give, the more I have. Thank you, Spirit!

June 12

Today I take a walk on the bold side. What wild ideas want to be unleashed in me? Today I let them out. First I admit them to myself. Then I write them down. Then I take the first steps toward their realization. As I do so, I am invigorated. I feel alive and passionate. Following bold ideas puts me in touch with the energy of creation. Building a relationship with this energy make me feel alive!

I am bold. I commune with the energy of Creation.

June 13

Taylor Swift was right. When you're stressed out, the best thing you can do is *Shake it off.*

Shimmy shimmy shake shake!

Moving my body moves everything. I shake my arms, and I feel tension fall off. I shake my legs, and I release pent-up anger. I shake my hands, and I feel joy and excitement rise in me. Today I remember the power of moving my body. When I allow myself to move freely, shimmying and shaking, it ignites movement in my mental, emotional, and spiritual bodies as well. Freedom! Release! *Yay!*

I shake. I shimmy. I am alive!

June 14

Peace begins with me.

It's that simple!

When I'm around someone who's in a dark and sad place, I leave feeling less vibrant and happy. But when I'm around someone who's joyful, I notice that I leave feeling uplifted. Our emotions are contagious. Today I practice the Presence and sink deeply into the peace that awaits me. I know that as I do this, I infect others with the energy of peace. As I surrender to my peace, I bless the world.

Peace is where I am today. I live in Peace.

June 15

Learning to pause before I speak is one of the most valuable gifts I can give myself – and others! I have all kinds of thoughts inside my head, but not all of them are worthy of being allowed to leave my mouth. Knowing what to say and what *not* to say gives me great power. Now I can cultivate love in the world. Now I can cultivate love in *myself*. Today I exercise my powers of speech and *non*-speech.

I value the miracle of silence today.

June 16

I live in a universe of abundance. Spirit did not put me here to shrink away. Spirit put me here to play, laugh, and enjoy my life. There's lots of "cake" in my life. Am I holding back from enjoying it? Am I waiting until I am "enough" in some area (finances/health/relationship status) before I let myself enjoy what is mine to enjoy? Time to stop waiting!

I enjoy the blessings of my life today. Today I eat cake!

June 17

I am much more than a task master. Yes, I can get things done, but if I forget to *be* in the middle of my *do,* I lose the best part. When I'm not *be*-ing, there's no one there to enjoy what I'm *do*-ing. Today I relish my *Be* and my *Do.* What a wonderful combination they are! As I *be* when I *do,* there is more of me present. And as I *do* when I *be,* I am more alive. *Do Be Do Be Do* is the best melody ever!

My life is a beautiful melody of *Do Be Do Be Do.*

June 18

My body is so smart. It knows what it needs in every moment. When I don't listen to it, it gets louder. As it gets louder, things can get out of balance. Today I practice listening to my body before it has to shout. *Hello, body. What do you need? Are you hungry? Do you need to rest? Do you want to move?* Whatever my body says, I listen and respond. The more I do this, the healthier I become. *Thank you, body!*

My body and I make a great team. I honor my body today.

June 19

Learning to love myself is a process. I may have been taught as a child that thinking highly of myself was bad. But self-love comes from Spirit. When I truly love myself, it is not vain or problematic. It is beautiful! There are so many ways to love myself. I can speak to myself with kindness. I can take sweet care of my body. I can let myself relax and take breaks. The more I love me, the more I love everything.

I love myself. I love others. I love the world!

June 20

Spirit is always available to help me. Sometimes the best way for Spirit to help is in the form of other people. Whom can I ask for help today? What project of mine would be aided by someone else's expertise? What questions do I have that could be answered by someone else's experience? When I ask others for help, I give them a great gift. They get to share and help someone. I give them that gift today.

I ask for help. I give a great gift!

June 21

Nothing is more beautiful than hearing someone who has discovered their own song. Whenever I feel timid or shy about who I am, I remember this. As more of us discover our unique songs, more of us sing our songs for the world to hear. As we sing out, we inspire each other to keep singing. To keep growing. To keep sharing. Our songs merge and harmonize, raising the vibration of the entire planet.

I sing out today. I inspire the world!

June 22

Behold! The Joy of an Unplugged Day!!

Technology is a miracle. Taking a break from technology is also a miracle! When I give myself time to step back from all sources of electronic communication, I allow myself time to connect with another amazing source of communication – me! When it's just me, parts of myself that may have been silenced can be heard. There is so much to learn in the realm of the unplugged. Today I listen.

I unplug. I connect. I listen.

June 23

It's easy to jump to conclusions about something. Especially something I don't understand. My mind loves to have answers and certainty, and it has no problem making stuff up! But when I pause, and stay curious about things I don't understand, I allow room for all *kinds* of new information. In this space of curiosity, my mind expands. I learn new ways of being in the world. I am never the same.

My curiosity expands my mind and my world.

June 24

Selfishness is defined as lacking consideration for others. But everything I do makes different people react differently. Today I am aware of what my inner guidance calls me to do. I understand that if someone doesn't approve of my choices, it is because of *their* wants. I check my motives, stay true to my inner guidance, and make choices that bless my life. I know that, ultimately, this serves everyone.

I allow others to be where they are. And I stay over here!

June 25

The best thing I can do for myself and the world is remember the power of Love.

Love can do anything. *Anything!*

Sometimes I get stuck. When that happens, I may think that the solution is a million miles away. But that's not true. Love is always here. *Right* here. And Love can do anything. *Anything*. Today, I remember the power of Love. I remember that I can call upon Love to help me in whatever I'm going through. Love can join me if I'm miserable. Love can also join me if I'm happy. Love is always welcome.

I welcome Love today. *Hello, Love!*

June 26

I'm a great driver. But I don't always know the best direction to go. When that happens, there's really only one thing to do: Let Spirit drive. Spirit always knows the best direction. Indeed, the more I'm willing to turn over the wheel to Spirit, the more I realize that it's better to simply let Spirit drive *all the time.* Yes, I'm still in the car. Yes, I still have a say. But Spirit is in charge.

I trust Spirit with my life. I am at peace.

June 27

Voices of authority are everywhere. Some I trust. Others I don't. Some I trust for a while, and then I don't. Staying in discernment about whom to trust is an incredibly valuable process. When I am awake and aware, I build a strong relationship with my own inner authority – Spirit. Ultimately, my connection with Spirit is what I trust. I relish this trust today.

I am awake and aware. I trust my connection with Spirit.

June 28

It's easy to be kind to someone when I first meet them. I haven't learned anything about them that bugs me yet! Once I really get to know someone, that's when kindness becomes a spiritual practice. Can I be kind even when I'm tired? Can I be kind even when I'm annoyed? Being kind – to loved ones *and* myself – is never the wrong thing to do. I will never regret an act of kindness.

I am strong enough to be kind today.

June 29

When we become aware that vicious cycles begin and end in the mind, we can change them.

Just say NO to Vicious!

Vicious cycles can appear to be outside me. A string of "bad" events happen, and it seems as though a trend has begun. But the only trend is in my mind. This is great news. I can stop those vicious cycles in their tracks (so to speak)! When I notice my mind creating a nasty cycle, I stop. I breathe. I affirm my good. I ask Spirit for help with all of it. Life is wonderful!

I say *No* to vicious cycles. I have the power to do this!

June 30

There have been many studies proving the power of prayer. Plus it just feels good! Today, I think of others with love. I know that as I do, I am increasing the love and goodness in their lives. I can send love any time of day, during any activity. I do this as often as I can. As I do so, love comes back to me and blesses my life. I am a blessing and I am blessed.

I send my love to the world today. I know it is received.

July 1

Health, wealth, and wisdom are mine. I may not always *feel* like they're mine, but they are! Today I notice all the ways in which I am healthy. I notice how my body supports and sustains me. Today I notice my wealth. I see the abundance all around me. Today I thank Spirit for the wisdom that lives inside me. Including the wisdom to notice how healthy, wealthy, and wise I am.

Thank God for my health, wealth, and wisdom!

July 2

Stuff happens. All the time. But the most important stuff that happens is what goes on inside me. My attitude can turn a small slight into a gigantic resentment. My attitude can turn an annoying problem into an invigorating adventure. The choice is mine. I have the power to turn my world into a nightmare or a celebration. I've had my share of nightmares. Today I choose to celebrate!

I celebrate my life. It gets better all the time!

July 3

Meditation can be challenging. There's so much noise out there. And there's so much noise in my head! Sometimes it feels like the heavily-caffeinated elephants are inside me, tromping and blasting, disrupting my chill and calm. Today I am grateful for the peace around me. Today I notice this peace and I take it within. I still the elephants inside. I appreciate the moments of peace in my mind.

I pause. I breathe. I am peace.

July 4

Singing with others is a unique experience. I take something intimate, the sound that begins inside me, and share it with others. Singing together has a calming yet energizing effect on the body and emotions. It's like magic. All I have to do is open my mouth and let it rip! Today I find ways to harmonize with others. As we "sing" together, our bodies and beings are blessed.

I am calmed and energized as I harmonize with others.

July 5

In a moment of crisis, it can be hard to see any benefits. But many of the "worst" things that happened to me brought new growth and opportunities. When I remember this, even in the middle of challenges, I open myself to a powerful perspective. Bad and good, black and white fade away. Spirit softens the sharp dichotomies. Blessings exist in everything.

I am always in the middle of a miracle. Thank you, Spirit!

July 6

Some things are easy to let go of. Others are a little harder. And then there are those things that I am absolutely unwilling to let go of. In that case, I may need to wait until I get *sooooo* tired that letting go is the only option. This isn't necessarily a bad thing. When I hold on to something for a super long time, I learn a lot. And the relief of letting go, when I finally allow it, is incredible. It's never too late to be free!

I let go when I'm ready. Freedom is mine!

July 7

When someone smiles at me, I smile back. The act of smiling releases the neurotransmitters dopamine, endorphins, and serotonin in my body, sending messages to my whole being that I'm happy. When I smile at someone else, and they smile back, I am bringing happiness to their body and being. It's such a simple way to be a blessing to the world.

I bring joy to the world by smiling at others today.

July 8

Spirit always tells the truth. When there are voices in my head telling me there's something wrong with me, that's not the voice of Spirit. Yes, there may be things about myself I want to change, but shaming myself is not the way to get there. Change comes with love, grace, and encouragement. That's what Spirit has to offer. I listen to Spirit's love today.

Spirit's truth lifts me up. I am encouraged today.

July 9

Sometimes I like to take a break from reading inspirational quotes and find my inspiration within.

I know. This is an inspirational quote. Embrace the paradox...

Inspiration is everywhere. It's in the people I meet. It's in the books I read. It's in the experiences I have. But when I forget that inspiration is also inside of me, I can become dependent on outside sources. That's when I need to pause and turn within. Having a strong connection with *myself* as a source of inspiration allows me to more fully appreciate *all* sources of inspiration.

I turn within and find my Source. I am inspired!

July 10

Today I focus on *sufficiency*. When I am coming from a place of lack, I feel like I can never get enough – not enough time, not enough money, not enough love. When I focus on sufficiency, I see how many of my needs are already being met. I see that I don't need to strive and stress to have enough, I only have to focus on what I need in this moment. And just like that, I am at peace.

I always have everything I need. I am blessed.

July 11

The life force within me is as powerful as the birth of a star and as gentle as the smile of a child.

Today I embrace my strength *and* my softness.

I am a badass. I can't help it! I am created and sustained by a force that births stars. That's as powerful as it gets. And, at the same time, there is great softness and gentleness in me. I can yield. I can wait. Today I celebrate my softness *and* my strength. I am guided and directed by Spirit to be strong in some moments, and soft in others. I trust this. And I trust the sweetness of my power.

I am strong. I am soft. I am Sprit's child.

July 12

One of the benefits of spiritual practice is that I can learn to stay mindful at all times - including during an argument!

Just because the moment is heated doesn't mean my mind has to be.

The more I connect with Spirit, the more I know that I am not my emotions. I may get agitated. I may feel overwhelmed. I may experience sadness. But this is not who I *am*. Spiritual practice helps me to cultivate a witness consciousness. As I witness my life and my emotions, I stay centered. No matter what happens, and no matter how I react, there is a part of me that is calm. That simply sees.

I witness my life today. I am awake and at peace.

July 13

Spirit is everywhere present. No matter where I am, or what I'm going through, Spirit surrounds me, enfolds me, and infuses my being. If I ever feel I've been abandoned by Spirit, I remember that, in reality, this is impossible. All I need to do is turn my attention to It. I ask for support and guidance. I breathe in the Divine. I allow myself to be held and loved by the nurturing Presence of The One.

Spirit is with me today, loving me with every breath I take.

July 14

In order to keep my momentum in any project, I know the value of moderation. When I stop a task when I still have energy to keep going, I can use that "extra" energy to pick up where I left off the next day. When I do this, I avoid burnout and cultivate a productive rhythm. This is great for getting things done, *and* it's great for my health and peace of mind. Yay me!

I pace myself today. I live in balance.

July 15

Listening to my intuition is the most powerful thing I can do.

Today I follow the best GPS ever: My heart.

Following instructions gets me where I want to go. When I listen to an electronic GPS, it takes me from Place A to Place B in the most efficient manner. When I listen to my *inner* GPS, it also gets me where I want to go in the best possible way. Unlike an electronic GPS, however, my inner GPS doesn't always give me access to all the steps ahead of time. I need to trust. But when I do? My life is a joy ride!

I listen to my inner GPS today. I enjoy the ride.

July 16

Love is magical. The more you give...

The more you have to give!

When I give something away, I should have less of it. But love isn't like that. Love transcends the normal rules of the material realm. With love, the more I give, the more I have. Indeed, when I make a practice to spend my days sharing love, my life becomes an overflowing testament to the mighty, magical power of love. Today I get myself in the flow of this mighty, magical power.

Love is magical. When I give love, I am magical too!

July 17

If I could look at a secret blueprint of my life, Spirit's touch would be all over it. Spirit made me. Spirit sustains me. When I bask in this knowledge, I realize that Spirit and I are inextricably joined. I can follow Spirit's lead in everything I do. I can ask Spirit for help whenever I am lost. I can marvel at the miracle of my life, sustained and supported by Spirit.

I am made by Spirit. I am a miracle!

July 18

Long-term goals are great, but they can be distant and elusive. When I finally attain them, the glory only lasts for an instant. But when I set small, daily goals for myself, goals that are in service of my larger goal and vision, then every day becomes a celebration. My enjoyment of daily accomplishments is a wonderful way to relish the journey.

I celebrate my accomplishments today. I love my life!

July 19

My old ideas got me where I am today. Today's reality is made of yesterday's stories, beliefs, and thoughts. Today I create a new reality. I keep what I love and cherish, and I release the rest. I bless my tomorrow by remaining conscious and aware of what I am creating. Today, I choose my thoughts with great care. Together with the Universe, I create tomorrow's greater good *today*.

I release old ideas today. I consciously choose my beliefs.

July 20

There is wonderful diversity in humanity. We have many different cultures, preferences, and experiences. And yet, no matter how different we are from each other, we are more alike than different. Spirit made each and every one of us. I am created and sustained by the same energy as my neighbor – and my "enemy." Today I remember the energy that unites us. I remember how much we have in common.

I am made of Spirit stuff. And so is everyone else!

July 21

Next time you're annoyed with the sounds of someone chewing ...

Imagine it's the Divine chewing. *Because it is!*

I have pet peeves. Everyone does. The next time I find myself in the middle of a peeve, I can remember that Spirit isn't annoyed by anything. In fact, Spirit *is* everything. So that thing I'm peeving about? It's Spirit! In fact, I can ask Spirit to help me see It in everything, even my peeves. How liberating!

I see the Divine in everything – even my peeves!

July 22

Everything changes. All the time. The only thing in my life that never changes is Spirit. Whenever I feel like life is too much to bear, I remember this. I remember that *This too shall pass*. And I remember that Spirit is with me in the passing. As I breathe into this awareness, I feel the hard edges relax. I feel calm. As I embrace the ever-changing nature of my life, I ground myself in Spirit's constancy.

I center in Spirit. I am grounded in the midst of change.

July 23

Cats are masters of self-satisfaction. They take impeccable care of themselves. Today, I follow the feline example. I practice loving myself. I practice feeling good about who I am. I remember that I'm the best me ever. I remember that no one is better at being me than I am. Indeed, even a superior, self-satisfied cat wouldn't be as good at being me as I am. Wow! I'm pretty cool. Now I know how cats feel!

I am doing a great job of being me. I'm *fabulous* at it.

July 24

I am a creative being. Today I *use* my creativity, starting with my mind. When I anchor my mind in the atmosphere of peace, it's amazing what happens. I see peace in myself and all beings. I experience peace and calm everywhere I go. I see harmony in my surroundings, even in the middle of "conflict." Peace is everywhere, and I know how to find it.

I breathe Peace. I envision Peace. I am Peace.

July 25

Having the ability to check my words before they escape from my mouth is a great gift to myself and others. Perhaps my words are true, but not kind. Perhaps they are both true and kind, but not necessary in a particular moment. In cases such as these, I can keep my words inside my mouth. They don't need to come out for air. As a result, my conversations are loving and respectful. Everyone wins!

True, kind, *and* necessary. That's how I roll.

July 26

The Universe has my back. How could it not?! The Universe *created* my back.

I am guided and protected every step of the way.

Quantum physicists now have scientific evidence of what mystics have been saying for thousands of years. There is one Cause behind and through everything. I am literally made of the same stuff as stars! Source creates me again and again, in each moment, with every breath. The Universe is loving me by giving me just what I need, over and over again. I am powerfully, deeply, and completely loved.

I am infinitely loved. All is well.

July 27

Following Spirit is good in *so* many ways. But three of them are especially sweet. 1. When I follow Spirit, peace prevails. Spirit's in charge, not me! 2. When I follow Spirit, my whole life gets better. After all, Spirit knows exactly what brings me joy, so following Spirit automatically brings more joy to my life. 3. When I follow Spirit, I build a deeper relationship with the Source of all. This intimacy enrichens everything.

I follow Spirit today. I am peaceful, happy, and alive!

July 28

Having a destination is wonderful. I know right where I am going and I feel satisfied when I get there. But having no destination at all is wonderful too. When I let myself wander, I discover new things – both in the world and about myself. When I wander aimlessly, my intuition comes forward. It guides me in each moment. Where do I want to go? Now where? And now? What fun I have!

I wander today. I discover the world.

July 29

Tom Sawyer attracted help painting his fence by pretending to be enthusiastic. But I don't have to pretend. When I follow my passions, my enthusiasm comes naturally. I can't help it! As I do what I love, I tap into the power of Spirit. In this place, the energy flows freely. It pours from me in the form of ideas and actions. And it comes back to me in the form of love and support. This cycle fuels my passion. What a joy!

I follow my passions today. I am in the flow.

July 30

What's the opposite of a vicious cycle?

A Blisscious Cycle of Never-Ending Good, of course!

As I learn to shift the vicious cycles in my head, a new pattern emerges. The shift away from vicious allows room for bliss. As the bliss gets rolling, and a new cycle is established, the momentum turns into something amazing: A Blisscious Cycle of Never-Ending Good. *Wow!* As I share my positivity with others, they are uplifted. They, in turn, uplift others. Watch out world, here comes Blisscious!

I cultivate positivity today. *Hello, Blisscious!*

July 31

Love is a trickster. It does magical and unexpected things.

Love – Surprise me today!

Love is my ally. There is no better force to align with than Love. As I align with Love, everything in my life is lifted up. New ideas come to me. Relationships are strengthened. I let go of old habits and replace them with better ones. And then there are the surprises, the shifts that come as Love works its magic in my life. I welcome all of it today.

I align with Love today. Best. Ally. Ever!

August 1

Moving forward means sometimes I stumble and fall. That's part of the process. When I realize this, I don't have to beat myself up for something that is a natural part of moving forward. What a relief! Now I can enjoy the process. Now I can even *enjoy* falling. It means I'm trying. It means I'm not afraid to make mistakes. It also means that I'm practicing my resilience, as I get up and keep going. Again and again!

I move forward. I stumble. I fall. I get up and I keep going!

August 2

*Hey you! That's right, I'm looking at you. You are soooo much cooler than you realize. You keep going, even when you feel like giving up. You make mistakes, and you learn from them. You uplift the people around you. So remember — don't be so hard on yourself. You're doing really well! You're being the best you **ever**, and you're getting better all the time. And you're cool. Did I mention that? Well, you ARE!*

I am cool. Today and every day. And I know it!

August 3

Nature is my role model. If I want to know how to stand tall, I look at a tree. If I want to know how to shine my beauty, I look at a flower.

I am strong and beautiful, just like my Nature Posse!

Nature is my perfect teacher. Luckily, I have access to it all year. Through the seasons, I witness nature's ever-changing glory. Nature is not afraid to shine its radiant colors and express itself with wild passion in every season. I follow nature's example today. It reminds me to be who I am, in all my unique and colorful glory. I shine my light and live my life full out with passionate self-expression. I am fully alive!

I shine my unique and colorful light today!

August 4

My monkey mind likes to jump from subject to subject, stopping just long enough to satisfy its curiosity, then rushing off to something else. My monkey finds this extremely satisfying. But when I'm trying to *meditate?* That's when I realize how hyper and unfocused the monkey can be! Using a mantra or counting breaths is a great way to focus my monkey. It allows space. Peace. Quiet. *Nice.*

I give my monkey a mantra. I give myself some peace.

August 5

Being mad is like being on drugs. My body feels a rush of adrenalin and my mind becomes compromised. Acting from this drugged-like state is usually not a good idea. Especially when it comes to verbal engagements. That's where breathing comes in. Taking a deep breath, and walking away when I need to, is a beautiful solution. I calm down, the drugs wear off, and I can speak from a place of peace.

Anger's not the boss of me. Breathing is!

August 6

If you're not sure what to do, just ask yourself: What would a Love-blasting unicorn do?

Then do that....

There are many pieces and parts to me. One of my favorite parts is the loving, sharing, magical-unicorn part. The part that likes to make others smile. The part that skips with joy and sings in the shower. Today I unleash the unicorn! When I'm not sure what to do, I ask myself what the happy, expanded unicorn part of me would like to do. I can never go wrong following the unicorn.

I am a Love-Blasting Unicorn. *I am!*

August 7

It's good to allow time in my schedule for both plugged and unplugged days.

I embrace the Plugged and the Unplugged!

There's a reason the fable of the tortoise and the hare is still around. It's a great story! When I pace myself and take sweet care of myself along the way, my productivity is increased. Today I take time for radical self-care. I know that as I do this, my future activity is more easeful. With ease comes accessibility to intuition, productivity, and greater joy. All this from *not* doing? Down time it is!

I allow myself rest. I come back stronger.

August 8

The best way to quiet the squirrely voices in your head? Send them love!

I love my inner squirrels!

The inside of my head can be a busy place. Squirrely little voices scamper around, vying for my attention. These voices say crazy things. Things like: *You're not good enough. There's something wrong with you.* Becoming aware of these voices is the first step. The second step is to send them love. The squirrels are run by fear. As I send them love, the fear dissipates. Only love remains.

Hello there, little squirrels! I love you!

August 9

I live in a world of duality. Black and white. Yin and yang. Male and female. But Spirit transcends duality. In Spirit, everything exists. And because I am made of Spirit, everything exists in me. I am masculine, I am feminine, I am everything in between. Stepping outside duality puts me in a rich field of infinite possibilities. I play in this field today. What can I discover about myself here?

I step outside duality today. I am All That!

August 10

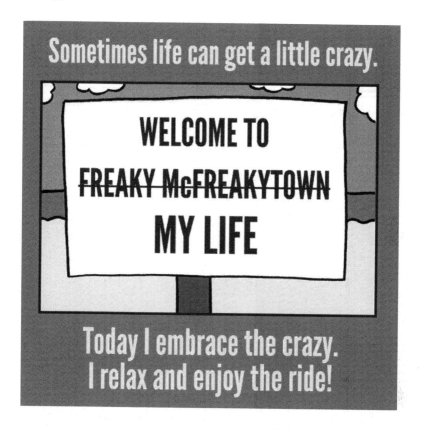

Sometimes life can get a little crazy.

WELCOME TO
~~FREAKY McFREAKYTOWN~~
MY LIFE

Today I embrace the crazy.
I relax and enjoy the ride!

Control is an illusion. Although I like to pretend I can control my life, I can't. That's why when I scramble to retain control, it makes me miserable. Today, I loosen the reins. I accept that Spirit's in charge. Accepting this truth can feel like a crazy ride sometimes. Unexpected and unwelcome events occur, sometimes on a daily basis. But I am safe. Spirit's got this. There is order in the "crazy."

I trust Spirit with my life. I am safe in the midst of "crazy."

August 11

Bringing awareness to my language changes my life. When I am unconscious about what I say, unhelpful thoughts and feelings are liable to escape. These thoughts and feelings create equally unhelpful circumstances in my life: lack, sadness, dysfunction. But when I deliberately cultivate positive speech? Watch out, life! Here comes growth, joy, and expansion. I love it. *Because I say so!*

I speak Truth today. My life shows it!

August 12

When I am hurt, it's tempting to lash out. I may want to tell the person who hurt me how bad I feel, or why they are wrong. But there's another option. When I simply say *Ouch*, I am communicating a big fat bundle of information without shame or blame. I am saying I am hurt. I am letting them know that something they did or said has elicited this reaction in me. And I am not lashing out. Perfect!

I communicate my feelings without shame or blame. *Ouch!*

August 13

Whenever you're feeling bad, it's because you're telling yourself a lie.

The Truth? You are magnificent. Beautiful. Loved by the Source that made you. That's the truth!

My emotions are great truth tellers. When I'm feeling bad, it's a wonderful opportunity to look at the thoughts behind my feelings. If I'm grieving, I simply need to let myself grieve. There's no way around it. But bad feelings are more often based on lies I'm telling myself *about* myself. Today I watch my thoughts. If I notice any lies, I counteract them with truth. Spirit can help me do this. Spirit *is* the truth!

I allow myself to tell the Truth today.

August 14

Sometimes things go smoothly. Sometimes they don't. But who's to say that one is *bad* and another is *good*? Actually, *I'm* the one who gets to say! Today I call everything *good*. If it's easy and smooth, great. If it appears to be an inconvenience, I find the humor in it. It's way better to laugh than to be annoyed. I feel better, and so does everyone around me.

I find humor in everything today. *Everything!*

August 15

Reading, writing, and arithmetic are great subjects for school. But what about affirmations? What about knowing our worth as children of the Divine? Today I envision every child in the world being told how incredible they are. I envision them knowing that they are made of Divine stuff. I also remind *my* inner child the same thing. As I do so, I feel a glow inside and all around me. The truth is beautiful.

I send my love to the children of the world. Including me!

August 16

I like to think I know a lot. And I do. But when I'm willing to admit how much I *don't* know, then I'm on the path to true wisdom. Today I question everything. Today I admit how little I know. Today I bask in the beauty of not knowing. What a relief to let go of having all the answers! What a relief to live in the question! When I do this, I make room for answers to come in magical ways. Today, I make room.

I don't know. *How refreshing!*

August 17

What do other people think of me? Do they like me? Do they approve of me? Actually, most people aren't thinking about me at all. I am number 538 on their list of concerns. *At best.* I'm often not on the list at all. If I think about it, they're often not on my list either! Today I throw out all the lists. I realize that the only opinion of me that matters is mine. What do *I* think of me? Today, I practice loving me.

Today I put myself first on the list. *I love me.*

August 18

If I'm experiencing a lack of love in my life, I know it's time to get centered. When I quiet down and notice the energy inside me, I am tapping into a source of love that is always available. And it's right here in me! The more I pay attention to it, the more I feel it inside me all the time. The more I feel love inside me, the easier it is to share it with others. Next thing I know, my life is full of love. And it started with me.

I feel Love. I share Love. My life *is* Love!

August 19

The middle of the night is a perfect time to pray for someone.

I send my love into the night and all is well.

Every moment is a perfect moment for prayer. When I'm waiting in line at a store. When I'm driving my car. Or in the middle of the night. As I send my love and light to someone else, they are uplifted. This energy always reaches them, whether they feel it consciously or not. We are all connected, and when I send love and light to someone, I strengthen that connection. Prayer is a gift to everyone. Any time!

I send Love and Light to others. We are all uplifted!

August 20

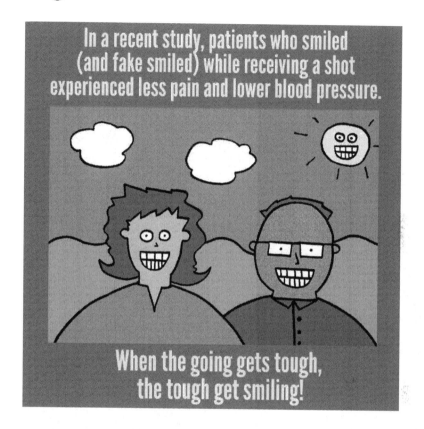

In a recent study, patients who smiled (and fake smiled) while receiving a shot experienced less pain and lower blood pressure.

When the going gets tough, the tough get smiling!

Smiling does wonders for the brain and body. When I smile, my blood pressure drops, my heart rate lowers, and feel-good endorphins are released into my blood stream. The endorphins released are also a natural pain-killers. So when I smile at others, their brain responds as if they're being rewarded. Because they are. By my smile!

Today I practice the art of smiling. Even if I have to fake it!

August 21

The stories I tell myself, combined with emotion, shape my reality. Today I tell myself happy stories. I enhance these stories with happy feelings, expanding and magnifying their power. As I allow myself to imagine feeling blown away by the wonder and glory of my life, I am drawing this wonder and glory into my future reality. It's the law!

I work with Spirit's laws today. I create an amazing life!

August 22

Not sure whom to trust?

Find Salvation HERE!

NO! It's in HERE!!!!

In the end, you need to build your own relationship with your Higher Power. That's why it's called *your* Higher Power.

Salvation is mine. All I have to do is build my own relationship with my Higher Power. If I turn over this relationship to someone or something else, I've lost my ground. It becomes difficult to know what to do or whom to trust. Today I remember the power and beauty of cultivating my own relationship with Spirit. There is no greater gift.

Salvation is mine. Mine and my Higher Power's!

August 23

Wow! My life is incredible. *Wow!* I thought I knew what I wanted. I thought I knew what was best for me. But Spirit had something even better in mind. *Wow!* I never would have predicted how amazing my life could be. And it keeps getting better and better every day. *Wow!* It's so wonderful to say *Wow!* and then let Spirit create a life beyond my wildest dreams.

Wow! My life totally rocks. *Wow!*

August 24

There are so many different rides to take. Every day, I have a choice to hop on a different one. The Vicious Cycle isn't one of the better rides. Each twist and turn gets worse and worse, until I find myself in a ditch, tired and miserable. And then there's the Blisscious Cycle. When I'm on this ride, each twist and turn brings new surprises. I feel joy, love, and expansion. It's so much fun! That's the ride for me!

I hop on the Blisscious Cycle today. What a great ride!

August 25

Learning to set boundaries is a process. At first, I realize I need to set boundaries because not having them is causing pain for me and others. Then, when I first set a boundary, it might not feel good. I might feel guilty and conflicted. But with time, I get used to setting boundaries. I see how effective they are. I see how they create freedom for me and others. And I wonder why I waited so long!

Boundaries, I love you. And you love me!

August 26

The older I get, the less I care what other people think of me.

Today I let my freak flag fly! I show my true self to the world and I am free!

There are so many different parts of me. There's a quiet, serious part. There's a loving, generous part. There's a powerful, energetic part. And then there's that *other* part. The part I've been embarrassed about. The part that I maybe got teased about as a kid, or that I'm afraid will be rejected when I reveal it to others. Today I love that part of me. Today I start to let it out. The world needs *all* parts of me.

I am free to be *all* that I am!

August 27

The sun is always out. But depending on how many clouds have decided to hang out in my corner of the sky on a particular day, I may not see the sun at all. In my *mental* atmosphere, however, *I'm* in charge of the clouds! My doubt, my fears, my anger – all of these serve to act as clouds, obscuring the pure light of my spiritual awareness. But the sun is always out. Spirit is always here. Today, I know this.

I clear the clouds today. I let Spirit's light shine!

August 28

My friends remind me that I am loved and that I belong. And I remind them of their belonging. Having friends is also a healing and powerful support for my dreams. Knowing I've got support behind me, I can go out in the world and take on scary new things, things that lead to my deepest desires. I nurture my friendships today. I am blessed and uplifted by the giving and receiving of love.

I give and receive love from my peeps today. I am blessed!

August 29

Random Meditation Thought #5486:
I'm the best meditator in the world.
I'm so good, I could teach an elephant to meditate.
That would be cool, to see an elephant in lotus position.
But what if they could get into position, and couldn't
get out?! What the $^%& would I do then?

Maybe I'm not ready for elephants yet...

When my meditation is going really well, my mind is free and clear. My thoughts slow down and I feel space in every aspect of my being. It's then that I'm aware of how *great* I am at meditating. I congratulate myself on my progress and start to count all the ways I have improved. Until I realize that my mind has become jammed full of thoughts again. And that's why they call it meditation *practice.*

I approach spiritual practice with humility. And patience!

August 30

Money is my friend. Money and I do wonderful things in the world. Sure, there are people who make up yucky stories about money. But I don't have to do that. I know that money is spiritual substance, as is everything in the world. Knowing this, I see money with the eyes of love. And I feel love back. We have a good thing, money and I! We like hanging out together and bringing joy everywhere we go.

Money and I make a great team. What fun we have!

August 31

Grumbletudes can be alluring at times. What's wrong with complaining a little? Especially when I feel like I've been wronged, or someone is being *especially* annoying. But Grumbletudes are like mice: they tend to reproduce at an alarming rate. Before I know it, I'm finding something wrong with *everything* in my life. There's only one cure: Gratitude. Today I scare away the Grumbletudes for *good*!

I chase away the Grumbletudes with my Gratitude.

September 1

Feeling frazzled? Take three deep breaths. *Right now!*

(You're welcome!)

I take a deep breath in. And I let it out. I take another deep breath in. And I let it out. I take yet another deep breath in. And I let it out. I am always breathing. As long as I'm alive, I am breathing in and out. But when I am *conscious* of my breath, and when I slow down enough to take a *deep* breath, it changes me. I am calmer. I am more aware. And I am ready to do whatever is in front of me.

I take deep breaths regularly. It wakes me up!

September 2

There's only one thing better than a good cry: how good I feel afterwards!

I allow the flow of feelings and tears. I am cleansed and made whole.

Even though some people equate crying with weakness, I know that the opposite is true. Being able to cry means that I am strong enough to allow all of my feelings, even the uncomfortable ones. Being able to cry means that I care enough about myself to allow all sides of me to express, including the tender, sensitive parts. Being able to cry means that I am open and responsive to my world.

I am strong enough to allow my tears.

September 3

The life force in me is creating new stuff all the time. At any given moment, I am manifesting big ol' trees *and* tiny seeds. Today I nurture the tiny seeds in me. What new ideas need nurturing? What new manifestations are wanting to burst through the ground, on their way to becoming big ol' trees? Today I am patient with my little seeds. I give them plenty of food, water, and sunshine. Spirit takes care of the rest!

I nurture my tiny seeds today. I love watching them grow!

September 4

When I'm hanging with a grumpy person, I pretend I'm playing tennis. After every negative comment, I hit a positive one back.

Either that, or I forfeit the match and get the heck out of there! Score: Love -- All

I am always humbled when I am hanging out with a grumpy person. After all, I have been that grumpy person at other times in my life. And even now, sometimes! So I treat grumpy people with love. I don't dive down into the grumbletudes with them, but I am kind. And positive. And unwavering in my positivity. *And*, if I need to, I walk away from grumpy with love. Love wins, every time.

I send love to the Grumpies today. Everyone wins!

September 5

My words reveal my beliefs. My beliefs create my life. As I choose and change my words, they work through layers of consciousness down to my subconscious, where my beliefs dwell. Today, I pay attention to what I say and how I say it. I notice the story behind my choice of words, and I notice how the story affects my attitude. If I need to, I change my story. As I uplift my words and my mind, I uplift my life.

I uplevel my words today. I uplevel my life!

September 6

There is no better guidance than that which comes from within me. My Higher Power is connected directly to Source. Indeed, it *is* Source. As I follow Source's guidance, life gets better and better. Today I practice the art of listening to the still small voice within. As I listen, the voice isn't still or small anymore. In fact, it's loud and clear!

The more I practice listening to Source within, the better I get at hearing it.

September 7

Being embarrassed isn't a bad thing. It's an opportunity to be more loving to myself.

I love all of me!

When I am embarrassed, I feel exposed. Some part of me has been uncovered, and it feels uncomfortable. This is a wonderful opportunity. The part that has been exposed is a part of *me*. And since it is a part of me, it deserves love. After all, Spirit made me, and everything Spirit makes is wonderful. When I realize this, I see that being embarrassed is a way for me to know *exactly* what part of me to love!

I love myself today. Every part of me.

September 8

Nothing feels better than throwing away something I don't need anymore.

I take out the trash today!

What do my surroundings look like? Are they cluttered and chaotic? If so, I take the time to clean things up. When the space around me is clean and tidy, I feel peaceful and relaxed. My mind and body are rejuvenated. In this space, new ideas can come. New growth can emerge. And then, if things get cluttered again, I take inventory and throw out or give away what I no longer need. Cleansing is empowering!

I clean up today. When my space is clear, I am clear.

September 9

The ego is like a drunk person. It says stupid stuff. All. The. Time.

I'm in charge, not Drunkie!

The contracted, egoic part of me is wrong a lot. *A lot!* And yet, because my ego is like an intoxicated person inhabiting my brain, it has no problem sharing its opinion with me. Often quite loudly. When I understand that this loud, inebriated part of me is usually in error, I don't have to take it seriously. I can step back, listen to its rants, and then follow Spirit instead. This clarity keeps me sane.

I follow Spirit today. Not Drunkie!

September 10

In a crappy mood?
Try singing your complaints!

♪ ♪
I'm in such a
bad mooooood!
♪ ♪ ♪

Shifts the energy a little, doesn't it?!

If I'm feeling bad, there's a really groovy thing I can do to switch things up. I can *sing* about my mood. It's one thing to think, *Everything sucks.* But when I sing *Everrrrry thiiiiiing suuuuuuuucks,* the energy changes. I can't help but smile, even a little. The music lifts me out of my mood. The more I sing, the more I am lifted. The music is always there, inside of me. When I tap into it, I tap into the Truth.

I let music lift me today. I open to its healing powers.

September 11

Nothing is stronger than Love. Nothing. When I forget this, things look scary. My world gets smaller and I stop trusting. When I remember the power of Love, everything comes together. The world looks brighter. I see possibilities in every corner. Not only that, I remember that *I* am also a source of Love. Love lives in me at all times, even when I forget it's there. Then I remember, and I am at peace.

Love lives in me. What a blessing!

September 12

Sometimes I lose perspective. I get so caught up inside myself and my problems, I can't see a way out. That's when other people come in really handy! When I talk to someone else, whether it's a friend, mentor, or counselor, they can see things I can't. Their objectivity can radically transform my perspective. Suddenly, I see solutions where I thought there were none. Asking for help saves me.

I am willing to ask others for help today. I am healed.

September 13

Every time I receive a criticism, especially if it's from a wearer of seriously-twisted knickers, I take a moment to consider the source. Are they really talking about me? Criticism leveled at me usually has nothing to do with me. If there is something helpful to pull from the critique, I use it to help me grow. But everything else? *Not mine*. I send love to the twisty knickers, and I let it go.

Today I let go of all advice that isn't really for me!

September 14

I have a folder in my mind of old ideas about myself: *I'm lazy. I'm shy. I'm never going to amount to anything.*

OLD IDEAS

I am a new person every day and I am amazing!

The ideas I hold about myself shape who I am. If I believe that I'm inept, I don't access the wisdom that lies within me. If I believe I am brilliant, I tend to think more clearly and make better choices. Today I check my ideas about myself. Have I been telling an outdated tale of woe about who I am? If so, I update my thinking. *I am in charge of the ideas in my head.* I cultivate awesome ideas about myself today.

I am brilliant. I am wonderful. I am powerful. *I am!*

September 15

Every success story includes failures that were overcome. It's just the way of things. It's a rare story that starts off with a dream and flies through to fruition without blocks and challenges along the way. That's just not how it happens. Today, I remind myself this. I remember that I never fail unless I give up. So I don't give up. I continue along my way to my goal's realization. Here I go! *Wheeeee!*

Failure only happens if I give up. I keep going today!

September 16

When I walk into new territory, I may feel afraid. The fear brings many questions. Will I be able to handle the new challenges? Will I be supported? Will everything turn out okay? The answers are always the same: *Yes. Yes. Yes!* Love has my back. Love has my front, middle, and sides. Love walks with me, Love cheers me on, Love will never leave me. It's okay to feel afraid. And I will always be comforted.

I move forward into the new. Love moves with me.

September 17

An army of Peace Warriors can transform the world.

I unite with my sisters and brothers in Peace!

As I strengthen peace inside and around me, I strengthen the energy of peace in the world. As I unite with others who are devoted to peace, our energy becomes a powerful force that heals and transforms the planet. Today I practice peace. I breathe peace. I speak peace. I send peace to everyone I encounter and everyone I think about. As I do so, I join with my sisters and brothers in peace. We are mighty!

I live in Peace today. I amplify Peace in the world.

September 18

I am great at creating. I have created a lot of wonderful things in my life – experiences and relationships among them. But the Universe is the greatest creator of all. It has all *sorts* of surprises up its Universal Sleeves. I have already been the blessed recipient of the Universe's surprises in my life. And there are more coming! I love that I'm not in charge of everything. I love knowing that glorious surprises await.

I delight in the surprises of the Universe!

September 19

I have so much good in my life. All I have to do is notice it! If there's a place where I'm not experiencing as much good as I'd like, the best thing I can do is focus on places where I *am* experiencing good. I appreciate what's going well in my life. I give thanks for all I have. I notice areas of growth and how far I've come. Next thing I know, more good is flowing in *all* areas. And all I had to do was appreciate what I have.

I focus on my Good today. There's so much of it!

September 20

Doubt and worry are the worst passengers *ever*. All they do is complain. They talk about all that could go wrong. They question every move I make. And they don't even offer to chip in on gas money! Today I kick these two lousy passengers off my ride. It's so much better without them. It's easier to move forward. I'm not constantly bombarded with negativity. And I get to actually enjoy the ride.

I kick doubt and worry to the curb. It's my ride, not theirs!

September 21

If someone has an issue with my true self, I know it has nothing to do with me. Whether someone loves me or hates me, it has nothing to do with *me*. They have an image of who I am and an experience of how they feel in relation to me, but all of that is happening over there, inside of them. And I'm over here, in me. *That's* where my connection with Love lives. *Whew!* What a relief. Now I can just be me.

Today I stay over here, where Love is!

September 22

Every day, I am confronted with new choices. What do I want to do? What do I want to say? Where do I want to go? If I'm ever in doubt, I can close my eyes and check in. Spirit is inside me, always available to help me in my decisions. I may meditate to hear Spirit. I may take a walk. I may simply check in with my gut feelings. However I do it, Spirit can guide me through all my choices. I am never alone.

I allow myself to be guided today. Spirit is right here.

September 23

The teenager I once was lives inside me. Sometimes, she feels afraid. She feels like she doesn't fit in. Today I remember this part of myself. I comfort her. I tell her that she's amazing, and that she is growing into an amazing adult. I remind her that she doesn't have to *do* anything to be loved. All she has to do is be herself. I give her a big hug today.

I love my inner teen. I give her lots of hugs today!

September 24

All of my problems start in my mind. I may have challenges. Things may change unexpectedly and I have to regroup. But nothing is a problem. Everything simply is the way it is. When I accept life exactly as it is, there is no problem. Today I practice radical acceptance. I look at everything and ask: How is this perfect just as it is? I embrace the answers that come. I embrace the perfection of now.

I have no problems today.

September 25

Humanity blooms in many forms. Like flowers, we come in a variety of shapes and colors. And, like flowers, we are all beautiful. Today I think about all the different shapes and colors of people on the planet. I think about what unites us. We all have worries. We all have things we cherish. And we are all adored by Spirit. I let my heart grow as big as Spirit's heart today. I cherish and adore the people of this planet.

I love the world with all my heart.

September 26

Nature knows what it's doing. It doesn't have to think about it. It doesn't need to have daily meetings to figure out how to make the streams run and the rains fall. Nature is a system, a system sparked and sustained by Spirit. When I go outside, I can feel this. I can feel the energy running through everything. I can feel this same energy running through *me*. My harmony with nature is my lifeblood.

I am Nature. And Nature is me.

September 27

Give a cat a fish? She eats for a day.
Teach a cat to fish? She eats for a day.*

* [She only did it to humor you.
It's never happening again.]

I am my own person. People may encourage me to do things. And I may try them out. But if it doesn't fit for me, I'm not going to keep doing it. What would be the good of that? I'm here to express my unique self. Everyone is! I enjoy being an example of the power of freedom and creativity. And I know I'm inspiring others to be and do the same. Like a cat, I do what I want, when I want. How awesome is *that?!*

I am a free agent. I do my thing and I love it!

September 28

In my life, I've had lots of dreams. Some of them have already come true. Some I let go of because they no longer fit. And then there are those other dreams, the ones that have yet to come true. As long as a dream makes my heart happy, I hold onto it. That happy-heart feeling is Spirit, manifesting inside me as a dream. Letting go of the dream is letting go of Spirit, and I'm not about to do that!

I love my dreams today. They are a gift from Spirit.

September 29

The more I focus on the love inside me, the more I see it all around me.

Love loves love!

I am a love machine! Love lives inside me all the time. Love pumps my blood. Love digests my food. Love comes up with new ideas and inspirations. Love reaches out to friends and lifts them up. When I focus on how much love is already inside me, it seems to grow. It flows from me out into the world, love greeting love. I love it! I am surrounded by love wherever I go. And it starts with me.

I am Love. I give Love. I receive Love. I love Love!

September 30

When a crazy idea passes through my mind, there's a tendency to dismiss it. *Nooooo. That's craaazy!* But, hold on. Why am I saying it's crazy? Because it might sound crazy to others? Because I don't want to take a chance? Today I make space for crazy. I let all my ideas roll around inside me, even the ones that seem completely nuts. In time, what started out as "crazy" may be the best thing that ever happened to me.

I make room for crazy today!

October 1

In the midst of chaos, all is well. In the midst of pain, all is well. In the midst of sorrow, all is well. Indeed, even when I'm feeling crazy good, but also wondering when the other shoe is going to drop and I'm going to feel bad again, all is well. Is there *ever* a time when all *isn't* well? Nope! Today I lounge in this knowledge. All. Is. Well. This is my set point, my absolute truth. I know it, and I live it.

All is well. All. The. Time.

October 2

There is one infinite energy that makes up everything in the Universe, seen and unseen. I am part of this energy, made of this infinite power. How can there be anything but awesomeness here? *There isn't!* Even as I continue to learn and grow, I honor the magnificent being I am. Today, I only listen to the truthful messages in my head.

I am Divine. Any other message is a lie. Truth? *I rock!*

October 3

Times of stress can cause me to lose perspective. My mind creates a magnifying glass, zeroing in on whatever is bothering me. Then all I can see is *that*. Today I shift my view. I take a step back and zoom out from my life. From a wider viewpoint, things retain their proper proportions. How important is that bothersome thing? In the bigger picture, *not very.*

I see the big picture of my life today. What a great view!

October 4

I love being kind. When I am kind, generosity fills my being. When I am kind, I tend to attract kindness from others. When I am kind, even when I encounter a grumpy person, I feel good because I treated them as sweetly and generously as I could. There are many things I could do or say that I would regret, but being kind isn't one of them. I will never regret being kind. Never!

I treat everyone with kindness today. Including myself!

October 5

Hello there! It's the Universe. I wanted to take a moment to address you directly. (I know — cool, right?!) There's something you need to know: I. Adore. You. Not like, I'm kinda fond of you and I put up with you out of obligation. Oh, no! I'm talking about a love as powerful as a trillion suns. BIG love. And it's unconditional. There's nothing you could ever do or say to lose my love. Can you let that in? Even a little? Good!

I am adored. Today I let this in as much as I can.

October 6

You are the sole resident of an amazing place: Your Life.

SUPER-AMAZING-INCREDIBLE LIFE

City Limits

Pop. 1 (YOU!)   Eleva. Unlimited!

Celebrate your life today!

My life is an extraordinary place to live. I reside at the center of a unique creation – *me!* I have my own tastes and preferences. I have my own talents and abilities. I also have the power to act on my preferences and abilities. In the process, I create things that have never been created before – experiences, dreams, relationships, passions. Today I honor my life. I honor the beautiful and powerful creator I am.

I celebrate my life today. *Yeeeee haw!*

October 7

Designated drivers have saved countless lives. Same goes for spiritual practice.

I let Spirit be my designated driver. I am free!

Thank God for designated drivers! There's no way to know how many lives have been saved by people being willing to abstain and care for others. The same is true for me and my spiritual practice. Sometimes I don't have the presence of mind to be driving the car that is my life. When I don't feel safe to drive, I turn the steering over to Spirit. Spirit knows the way. I surrender and find peace.

I let Spirit drive my life. I am at peace.

October 8

I love looking to others for inspiration. When I step outside myself and look at the lives of others, I see things in them that I can't always see in myself. When someone makes a mistake and then gets up and keeps going, I don't condemn them for falling. Instead, I celebrate their patience and perseverance. It reminds me that I can do the same when I fall. The resilience of others inspires my own.

I watch. I learn. I am inspired!

October 9

Touch is a gift. When I hold the hand of someone I love, I am comforted. When someone I love is in need of support, I take their hand in mine. I give and receive love simply by holding the hand of another. It's so simple! And yet it can have such profound, positive benefits. When someone is really hurting, or when that someone is me, it can be hard to know what to say. Touch says it all.

I hold the hands of those I love. We heal each other.

October 10

My mind can be a drama queen. It takes a small piece of information and blows it up to epic proportions. Proportions that are always disastrous and worst-case-scenario. And then it won't stop talking about it. Or screaming about it. Today I tell the drama queen that she has a new title: The Best-Case-Scenario Storyteller. Now she can use her powers for good. Everyone wins in this story!

My mind tells wonderful stories today.

October 11

Ever hidden a part of yourself?

Remember, there's more support available when you stop hiding. Come on out and let in the love!

When I'm making a part of myself wrong, I want to hide it away. I don't want anyone to know about it, not even me. But Spirit knows. Spirit knows everything about me and loves me just as I am. When I reveal hidden parts of myself, I am allowing Spirit to love me more. Now Spirit can show up in the form of other people loving me too. And as I share all parts of myself, *I* love me more.

I am willing to come out of hiding today.

October 12

At the end of each day, find something that you did particularly well. (Even if it's just getting out of bed!) Then give yourself an A+ for a job well done.

You're doing good!

Looking back on my day and finding things I did well is an empowering practice. It helps set up a positive momentum in my life: *Look what I did. That's great! Let's do some more cool stuff!* When I celebrate my successes, it makes me eager for more. Today I notice what I do well. I give myself props as often as I can. As I do so, I notice that I'm more apt to give others props as well. Positive momentum indeed!

I give props freely today. It feels great!

October 13

Having to choose between two different paths can bring up lots of questions. Sometimes these questions help clarify my choice. Other times, they confuse the issue. If I'm confused and I'm not able to wait to make my choice, that's a great time to *feel* into my decision. Which choice makes me feel more alive? Which choice feels both expanded and peaceful? *That's* the choice for me!

I feel into my choices today. I trust my gut.

October 14

I've got a great gig. I get to strut around on the stage of my life, singing my heart out. The Universe, meanwhile, is backing me up on drums, guitar, keyboards – even a horn section. What rockin' music we're making! Today I remember to claim my role at the center stage of my own life. I remember that the most compelling rock stars are those that really *go for it*. That's me. That's what I do!

I rock my life today. And the Universe backs me up!

October 15

Fat Ankle Syndrome: The tendency in romantic relationships to maximize small undesirable traits .

The payoff? You get to stay separate and "safe." How's that workin' for ya?

I don't like everything about everybody. That's part of being human. But when I spend my time focusing on things in others that I don't like, I tend to attract more negativity into my life. On the other hand, when I focus on the traits in others that I enjoy, I attract more joy. It's pretty simple! The trick is to keep focusing on the positive, even when my mind wants to stray into Fat Ankle Land.

I see the good in others. My world is better for it!

October 16

It's healthy to be skeptical sometimes. After all, not everything presented to me is what it seems. But once I learn how to listen to Spirit, and once I get clear about what Spirit is saying to me, it's a good idea to listen. I don't *have* to listen, of course. And sometimes I don't! But time and again, I find that Spirit's vision for me is always amazing. Often more amazing than anything I could imagine!

I stop arguing today. I let Spirit win the debate.

October 17

Comparison is a down payment on suffering.

YOU	ME
1. More Facebook friends	1. Not as good as you
2. More Facebook likes	2. Not as good as you
3. Better Facebook pictures	3. Not as good as you

I embrace my unique and incomparable self!

Comparing my insides to someone else's outsides is a losing proposition. Of course they look better than me! I have no idea what their life is really like. When I look only at the surface of how someone else *seems* to be, and then make myself worse in comparison, I set myself up for needless suffering. Today I cut that out! I embrace the amazing person I am. Who would I rather be? No one. Just *me!*

I am *wonderful*. I love my wonderful self today.

October 18

Hurling love is a great hobby. Whom can I share love with today? Maybe it's the clerk at the store. Maybe it's a co-worker. Maybe it's a friend who's feeling low. Maybe it's me! When I throw love all over the place, there's more love in the world. Plus I'm strengthening my love muscles, which builds even *more* love in me. What a powerful practice! It should be in the Olympics. I'd win a gold medal!

I am mighty Love hurler today. I fill the world with Love!

October 19

When I expect the world to be safe and friendly, it is.
When I expect otherwise, I experience otherwise.

The choice is mine: What kind
of world do I choose today?!

When I expect my day to suck, it usually does. Today I watch my expectations. Today I choose to anticipate a magical, wonderful day. I thank Spirit for aligning the entire universe in my favor. I am excited to see the fabulous surprises that await. I am grateful in advance for my fantastic, fun, productive, amazing day. And look! Here it comes! *Ooooooooh.*

Today is amazing, fun, productive, and fabulous. *Wow!*

October 20

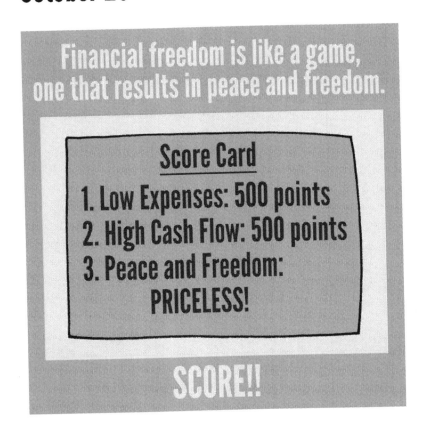

Financial freedom is like a game, one that results in peace and freedom.

Score Card

1. Low Expenses: 500 points
2. High Cash Flow: 500 points
3. Peace and Freedom: PRICELESS!

SCORE!!

Financial freedom is a two-part process. The first part is aligning with abundance in my mind and heart. The second part involves working with money in the world. Today, I cultivate both parts. 1. I open to abundance, doing what I can to allow a flow of money into my life. 2. I am smart with my finances. I spend money wisely and consciously. Working both these parts buys me freedom!

I cultivate financial freedom. I cultivate peace.

October 21

The sun isn't worried what anyone else thinks about it. It's not holding back its fiery greatness so that other suns won't get jealous. It shines powerfully and radiantly all the time. I take my cue from the sun today. Holding back my light doesn't serve anyone. Indeed, when I hold back, I'm depriving those who would be nurtured and inspired by my radiance. I let myself shine today.

Hello, sun! **Let's do some shining today!**

October 22

Spirit lives deep inside me. Spirit also lives everywhere and in everything. One of the beautiful ways Spirit shows up outside of me is in the form of friends. In my life, I have had different kinds of friendships. Some have lasted a long time. Others were much shorter. But every single friend I've ever had has enriched my life. And I've enriched theirs. Friends are a treasure. I celebrate my friendships today.

I am grateful for my friends. They complete me!

October 23

Hello, there! It's Spirit, giving you a call. How's your day going so far? Great? Not so great? Well, here are some flowers for you! Flowers are always a wonderful idea — for good times and not-so-good times. I want to give you flowers because I'm a not-so-secret admirer of yours. I know it feels like a secret to you, when you forget how much I love you. But today I want you to remember: I love you. I adore you. And that's the Truth.

Today I accept the gift of Spirit's love.

October 24

Even the most well-meaning people can misguide me if I let their opinions override my inner knowing. While others can support me in finding my way, it is ultimately *my* way. Today I take the time to find it! If others give advice, I pay attention to how it feels. How does my inner knowing react to what they are saying? I stop and listen deeply, knowing I am never mislead by my intuition. I follow it today.

Today I take advice from an expert. *Me!*

October 25

Know what you're better at than anyone else on the whole planet?!

Being you.

There are lots of things it's taken me a long time to get good at. Walking took practice. Learning to talk and read also took some doing. And then were all those other skills, abilities I needed to function and work in the world. But there's one thing I don't need to practice at all. And that's being me. I do it naturally! I do it all the time, every day. Today I celebrate the wonderful *me* that I am.

**I am awesome at being me. I am the best me *ever!*

October 26

Saying "I don't know" is one of the most powerful things you can do.

I am willing to sit in the question.

I don't know what's going to happen tomorrow. As I navigate life as a conscious creator, this can feel disconcerting. Today I ask Spirit to help me move past my discomfort. I open to a deeper trust in the Divine Love that created me. I remember that I am safe in the unknown. I remember that Spirit brings me answers at the perfect time. All is well.

I am safe in the unknown. Spirit has me.

October 27

When I remember how powerful my words are, I'm more conscious about what I say. Today I watch my words. I make a conscious choice to use positive and empowering language, both about myself and others. When I catch myself straying into negativity, I stop and start over. One awesome thing about language is that it doesn't cost anything to speak positively. And the rewards are infinite!

I speak with the power of positivity today.

October 28

Next time you think you're caught in a vicious cycle, remember...

It's just a goofy little bicycle with no spokes and bad teeth!

Vicious cycles can feel overwhelming. One cruddy thing after another. *Yuck!* Today I hold my vicious cycles lightly. I imagine funny little bikes in need of some serious dental work. When I do this, I'm using the power of my imagination to remind me where vicious cycles live – in my mind. My mind can shift *anything*. The funny little bikes are my cue to turn vicious cycles into a blisscious ones.

Bye-bye, **wacky little bicycle! I choose Blisscious now!**

October 29

When our path is blocked, it's because the Universe has something better in mind.

CLOSED

I celebrate the detours in my life. I await their gifts with joyous expectation!

Detours are Spirit's way of working magic. It might not feel like it in the moment. It might feel like I'm being thwarted. But that's never the case. Whenever my plans appear to be blocked, I can be assured that Spirit is at work, coming up with something better than what I had in mind. Today I remember to trust Spirit's timing. I trust that what appear to be "detours" are Spirit's way of loving me.

I love my detours today. I let them work their magic!

October 30

Everyone is made of Love. Whether they know it or not.

I practice seeing everyone with the eyes of Love today.

Seeing everyone with the eyes of love can be challenging. But here's a little trick. Before I attempt such a mighty feat, I align myself with the power that made me. That power is ... Love. Right?! So when I turn my attention to others, I let Divine Love help me see them with love. This makes my job much easier. I don't have to effort. I don't have to force it. I simply ask Love to help me. And Love always does.

I see everyone with Love. Love helps me do it!

October 31

How can I be even more of myself? Is that possible? Today I explore the ways. As I grow older and wiser, I'm finding more and more avenues to express my true essence. When I was younger, folks around me told me what to do and who to be. Now, even when that happens, I know I don't have to listen. I can be myself, at all times and in all ways. I am an original. I express my original essence today.

I celebrate who I am today. *Yipeeee!*

November 1

Meditators are everywhere. When I see a cat sitting quietly, staring into space, I am reminded of the power of quiet contemplation. When I see a tree standing tall, leaves billowing in the breeze, I remember the power of standing tall in the breeze of life's changes. Going within and finding my inner stillness is one of the best gifts I can give myself. Like the cat and tree, I find power in the stillness.

Meditation is a superpower. I access it today!

November 2

When tension and strife enter the picture, I can get discombobulated. That's when it's time to center myself in peace. I may have to remove myself from the situation for a while, or I may choose to stay put and breathe my way back to center. Once I get there, I perpetuate the peaceful vibe by speaking from the peace inside me. As I speak peace, it moves from me out into the world. I watch it grow with gratitude.

I speak from a center of Peace today.

November 3

One of the best things I can affirm for myself is that everything keeps getting better. As I do this, I am making room for Spirit to bring wonderful new things into my life. These new things may be different than what I expected. But because I'm affirming that things keep getting better, the new surprises augment my life in wonderful ways. And then? Everything keeps getting better and better!

Every day, in every way, my life gets better and better.

November 4

Big challenges can be daunting. *Can I really do this? What was I thinking?* Doubt at the beginning of a challenge is natural. But I don't have to do everything all at once. I only have to take one step at a time. As I do, clarity comes. I see the next steps in front of me. My confidence grows. Before I know it, I'm skipping along, having forgotten about my doubts. All because I heard them and then moved forward anyway.

I got this! And Spirit's got it with me!

November 5

Worrying what other people think is like standing on an ever-shifting sea.

Today I leave the changing tides for the solid ground of knowing my own worth.

Other people are always going to have opinions about me. Some people will celebrate who I am and what I do. No matter what. And some people will criticize who I am and what I do. No matter what. Today I follow my own inner knowing and allow myself to shine my bright light in the world. I do what is right for *me* to do. I allow myself to be who *I* feel good about being.

I have my own inner compass. I allow it to guide me.

November 6

I can never break up with Spirit, but sometimes I try. Maybe I tell myself it's too hard to be on a spiritual path. Or maybe my doubt rises to the surface, convincing me there's no such thing as a Higher Power anyway. But no matter how many times I *think* I'm pulling away from Spirit, It's always here. It's always loving me, even when I'm full of doubt. I relax into this knowing today.

I am loved. Always.

November 7

Washing away a bad mood can be as easy as washing your hair.

Next time you take a bath or shower, visualize the water carrying away your stress...

Water is a powerful healer. When I bathe and shower, water cleans my body and leaves me feeling refreshed. The water also cleanses my energy, clearing out tangled emotions and helping to order my thoughts. Today I give thanks for water. I give thanks for all the ways it cleanses me. When I'm in a bad mood, I consciously give my troubles to the water and allow it to wash them away. I am cleansed and made whole.

Thank you, water! I allow you to heal me today.

November 8

I allow myself to breathe and stay present today. I am safe in the world because I take care of myself. I listen to my inner knowing and I don't go where I am not safe. I use all my inner and outer resources to take care of me. As I do so, I know that the present moment is a safe place to be. The more I take care of me, the more I stay in the here and now.

I am safe, in me, now. I am fully present today.

November 9

Attitudes and emotional vibrations are contagious. Some say that angels, sent to this plane to help, do their thing and get out as quickly as possible. The energy here is too dense for them. Sometimes the fields in which others vibrate are too dense for me. If I'm around them for too long, I feel negative about life and myself. Today I manage my own energy field by carefully managing my time with others.

I am selective about whom I spend time. I am nice to me!

November 10

There's only one thing happening here. One power and presence in all of creation. This presence births planets and stars. It makes mountains and oceans. And it also makes *me*. *Wow*. That's incredible! Today I remember what I'm made of. I remember that this presence is guiding and sustaining me in every moment. And I remember that I can call upon this presence for comfort when I need it. What a *gift*.

I am soooooooo blessed!

November 11

Coming together with others for a bigger purpose lifts my spirits. I may sit with others in a group meditation. I may march with others for justice and freedom. I may join with others to sing and dance. As I merge into the collective energy, I feel my own energy rising. Where two or more are gathered, awareness of Spirit is amplified. I am healed by this amplification. The planet is healed.

I join with my brothers and sisters in Spirit.

November 12

Driving can bring out the worst in people – including me! The next time I notice myself getting crabby behind the wheel, I practice saying kind things to other drivers. I may have to speak sarcastically at first – but it doesn't matter. The power of words like *love* and *forgive* transcends the sarcasm. Next thing I know, I'm smiling. I'm feeling more compassionate toward the other drivers. And myself.

I practice love and forgiveness on the road. All roads!

November 13

There is nothing like getting outside and breathing fresh air for restoring mental clarity. Time in nature also supports memory, combats mental fatigue, and lowers my stress hormones. The physical and mental benefits of the great outdoors can even do their thing when I can't get outside. All I need to do is look at *photos* of nature and I am renewed! I let myself be healed by nature today.

I breathe in the beauty of nature today. I am healed.

November 14

All of us are a blend of masculine and feminine traits. The key is to embrace this fact, not condemn it.

I embrace all of me!

There are many different sides to me. There are parts that like to be active and engaged. Other parts like to be quiet and soft. Some people call different parts masculine or feminine, and it may empower me to label them as such. Or not. Either way, when I let *all* parts of me express, I am more completely me. I am more completely expressing the gifts and traits Spirit gave me. Spirit embraces all genders.

I express myself fully today. Spirit loves all of me!

November 15

Entertainers like Catvis Purrsley remind me that there is great value in being entertained. Joy is an expression of the Divine, and finding ways to feel joyful is a powerful pursuit. What makes me happy? How can I bring more joy into my life? These are my questions for today. As I open to more joy, I welcome answers from both expected and unexpected sources. After all, surprises are yet another source of joy!

I am a lean, not-so-mean Joy-Seeking Machine!

November 16

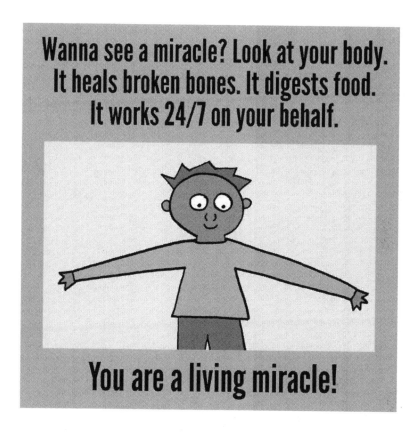

Wanna see a miracle? Look at your body. It heals broken bones. It digests food. It works 24/7 on your behalf.

You are a living miracle!

My body is working all the time. When I'm sleeping, when I'm awake, even when I'm spacing out, doing nothing at all. My body is *on* it! When I injure a part of myself, my body immediately starts the healing process. My body is a *miracle*. Whenever I feel like I'm not supported in this world, all I have to do is look at my body. My body is supporting me all the time. *All. The. Time.* Thank you, body!

I am living in a miracle. What a blessing!

November 17

New beginnings are exciting. I walk through a new door and everything changes. One part of my life shifts, and everything else shifts in response. Today I remember the power of reaching out for help when I start something new. The encouragement of others keeps me going when the new shifts get overwhelming. I remember that I'm not alone. Then, when the time comes, I encourage others as well.

I allow myself to be encouraged today!

November 18

Sometimes I have a strong sense that something isn't for me. It's a *Hell No.* Other times, it's the opposite: Something is *definitely* for me. *Hell Yes.* But what about when it's neither? Today I embrace the *Hell Maybes.* Not everything is clearly one or the other. As I allow *Hell Maybes* to be what they are, I welcome Spirit into the conversation. In time, clarity comes. Inviting Spirit to help is always a *Hell Yes!*

Do I want to allow Spirit's clarity into my life? *Hell Yes!*

November 19

Sometimes sending someone a loving thought is the best way we can help them.

I send my peeps lots of love today.

I love helping people I love. But sometimes I can't help. They may not want my help. They may reject my help when I try to give it. Or I may sense that giving them help directly is not what the situation calls for. In all those cases, I can still help. I can send them love. I can send them light. I can imagine them as gloriously happy and fulfilled. This is *always* a good thing to do. And it uplifts me too!

I blast my loved ones with positive vibes today.

November 20

I can't feel both optimistic and pessimistic at the same time. So today I continue my ongoing practice of guiding my thinking back to the positive. As I do so, I am less able to hear the Grumbletudes. Pretty soon, I forgot what they were clamoring on about in the first place. My mind is a center of Divine creation. I do my part today. I focus on the good.

I focus on the good and find more of it!

November 21

When I'm up against a deadline, time can feel like an enemy. It feels like it's crushing down me, restricting my ability to breathe and think clearly. That's when it's time to tap into Spirit. In Spirit, there is an endless amount of time. In Spirit, there is an endless amount of *everything*! When I'm in this space, I start to relax. I breathe deeply. And, magically, I find the space, time, and resources to do what I need to do.

I have everything I need to do everything I want.

November 22

Affirmation Envy (definition): The concern that everyone else's affirmations are bigger, brighter, and more effective than yours. The only cure for Affirmation Envy? Affirmations!

My affirmations rock! My affirmations are empowering my life to be even better than I ever would have imagined!

Everyone has their own spiritual path. And yet sometimes I look at others and think they're doing a better job at it. *Nope!* My affirmation/meditation/yoga envy is simply my pesky mind, playing tricks on me. My affirmations are perfect for me! So is my meditation practice and everything else. When I feel myself getting pulled off course by comparison, I center myself back in Spirit. *Ahhhh. Envy, what envy?*

Spirit guides my spiritual practice. It's perfect just as it is.

November 23

Grumbletude turns my life into a dark and cloudy place. Everything looks gloomy and gray. I worry that the sun will never come back. Gratitude, on the other hand, brings out the sunshine. Everything looks so bright and sparkly and beautiful. The wonderful thing about grumbletude and gratitude is that I am always at choice. In every moment, in every day, I choose my view. Today I choose gratitude.

I am grateful for gratitude today. My life rocks!

November 24

Plans are beautiful things. They give me structure and help me move forward. But plans are ultimately just that – *plans*. They're theoretical constructions, and when my plans meet reality, reality always wins. Today I give thanks for reality. I give thanks for the feedback it provides. I get to see which parts of my plan worked, and which parts need updating. I may *call* the updates "mistakes," but I'm really just learning.

Thank you, reality. You're teaching me so much!

November 25

When I fill my head with good vibes, there's less room for crappy stuff.

I fill my head with love today!

I get to fill my head with whatever I want. When I put positive and affirmative stuff in there, my life shines. But sometimes other things like to camp out in my head – old ideas and images of myself and other people. When I find one of those old ideas, I surround it with love. I recognize that it was trying to help and protect me, and now I gently let it go. It feels so good to have a head full of love!

I love myself. I love others. I love everything!

November 26

Spirit is my guide. I give my life over to Spirit's direction. Because of this, I am sometimes guided to go in a direction that no one else understands. They may urge me to go an "easier" way. But when I go against Spirit's direction, it's anything but easy! All my good lies along the path where Spirit leads me. I trust this today. I trust myself and my relationship with Spirit. In this, I am richly blessed.

I follow Spirit today. I watch my Good unfold before me.

November 27

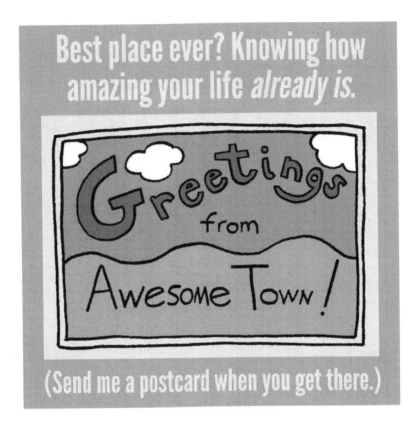

I am a powerful creator. With Spirit's help and guidance, I am continually making my life better and better. It's fun to do this. It's empowering. But if I get too caught up in what's emerging, I sometimes forget to appreciate what's already here. Today I appreciate all that I have. All that I *am*. Wow! Spirit is right here with me, and my life is *amazing*.

I live in Awesome Town. *Best. Place. Ever!*

November 28

When I step away from the screens in my life, I am stepping away from other people's views of reality and anchoring myself more fully in mine. The things I can discover here are endless! It's like my life suddenly expands, and I can see all sorts of things that may have been hidden in my day-to-day screen routine. What does Spirit want me to know about my life? What new perspective awaits? Today I find out.

I step away from the screens. I discover myself.

November 29

The more I allow myself to be still, the more I feel the love that lives in me.

I love the love inside me!

Sometimes I need to stop and just *be*. With practice, I get better at quieting the inner chatter and finding stillness within. In the stillness, I can rest in the midst of Divine Love. I can merge with all of creation. And I can find peace. Today, I allow time for restful stillness. I allow time to be the Love that I am. And I reap the rewards.

I find the stillness within, where Love dwells.

November 30

Ever had your boundaries trampled on like a herd of caffeinated elephants were escaping from the circus?

Remember: It's never too late to say *No*.

Having my boundaries violated is not one of my favorite things. There are lots of ways I'd rather spend my time! That's why the word *No* is so fantastic. I can say *No* to anything. I can say *No* at any time, even if I said *Yes* in the past. I am in charge of my life, and I get to choose what I want to do and whom I want to spend my time with. Do I want to the elephants to come over? *No, thank you!*

I say *No* today. I am free!

December 1

Setting goals is a great motivator.

Things To Do Today

- ☐ Get Out of Bed
- ☐ Get Dressed
- ☐ Eat
- ☐ Win Olympic Gold Medal

If we don't achieve all the goals on our list, we can just make a new list. *Next!*

Setting goals is a great way to get myself mobilized. Setting goals in alignment with Spirit is an even better way to get myself mobilized! Sometimes I may set very specific goals and Spirit helps me attain them. Other times my goals may be more fluid, and Spirit helps me fill in the details as I move forward. However I do it, Spirit is always there as the ultimate goalkeeper!

I move forward with Spirit. We always meet our goals.

December 2

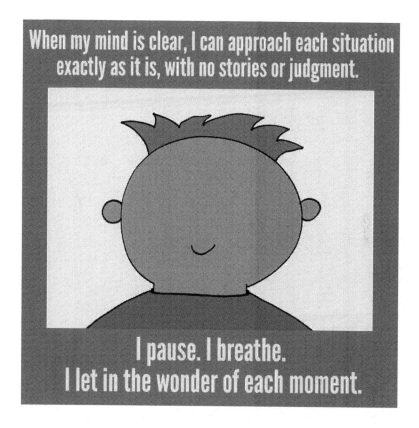

When my mind is clear, I can approach each situation exactly as it is, with no stories or judgment.

I pause. I breathe.
I let in the wonder of each moment.

A clear mind allows me to see all kinds of things I might otherwise miss. When my mind is full, everything I see is from the lens of cluttered thinking. But a clear mind allows me to *see*. Today I cultivate a clear mind. I look at everything as if I am seeing it for the first time. I activate all my senses in appreciation of the sights, sounds, fragrances, and textures around me. It's so beautiful! Today I *see* it.

I open my mind and see the world.

December 3

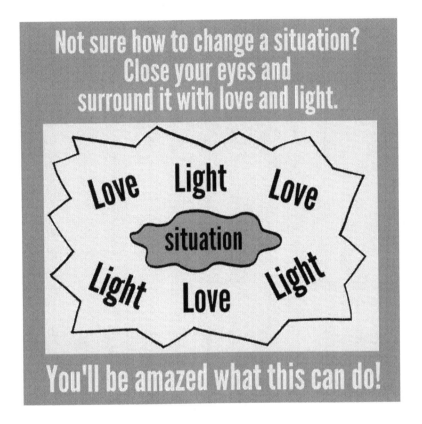

Not sure how to change a situation?
Close your eyes and
surround it with love and light.

Love   Light   Love

situation

Light   Love   Light

You'll be amazed what this can do!

Problems seem to require solutions. But what if all they need is a new vantage point? When I surround a "problem" with love and light, I am transforming it. In my mind, it becomes a thing of beauty. Look at all that sparkly light! Look how it softens my "problem" and makes it shine! Every time I think of a "problem" today, I surround it with love and light. In this beautiful practice of surrender, miracles are born.

Love and Light are what I am. I share them freely today!

December 4

Stretching beyond my previous versions of myself can be scary. But it can also be exhilarating! Sometimes, the only difference between those two experiences is my perception. Today, I listen to the part of me that says I can be more – more of me. I allow myself to stretch, knowing that Spirit is right here with me, *in* me. Taking me flying!

Today I follow Spirit's lead. I stretch into the next greater expression of *me*.

December 5

Any time I'm feeling crappy about myself, I can be sure that I forgot something. I forgot how totally, absolutely, undeniably *incredible* I am. Spirit made me. I'm a one-of-a-kind creation of the Divine. I'm a living, breathing miracle! When I remember this, I stand up straight and smile. When I remember this, I feel great. Why? Because I'm in harmony with the Truth. And the Truth feels *amazing*.

I am a rockin' and rollin' creation of the Divine!

December 6

Today I am kind. I am kind to my body. I do all I can to keep it healthy and strong. I am kind to my mind. I allow it to rest when it needs to. I nurture it with stimulating ideas and activities. I am kind to my emotions. I allow them to flow freely through me, without stuffing them away. As I am kind to myself, my kindness naturally moves from me into the world. I am kind to everyone I see. Rule Number 1 rules!

Kindness is the way, the truth, and the life.

December 7

Acting *as if* is a magical tool. At first, I feel like a fraud. I'm just pretending. I'm sure no one will believe me. But they do! People start treating me differently. *I* start treating me differently. Little by little, my insides change to match the way I am acting outside. Before long, I'm no longer acting *as if*. I'm just being me! Acting *as if* gives me the courage and structure to become more of who I really am.

I act *as if*. I become myself!

December 8

When I'm fearful about money, no amount is enough.

I relax into abundance today!

Fear makes every part of me contract. When I'm afraid, I can't relax. I burrow into a little hole where I lose touch with Spirit's abundant life. Today I relax. I breathe and let my shoulders drop. As I relax my body, I am aware of how supported I am. Gravity holds me on this precious planet. There's plenty of air for me to breathe. And there's plenty of Spirit's love and abundance. I let it in today.

I relax into the Truth today. I am abundant!

December 9

The moments after I wake up are fertile ground. It's a wonderful time to plant seeds that grow and bloom the rest of my day. Inspirational readings are a fabulous thing to add to this mix. One idea from a reading can catch hold of my imagination and take off, leading me to brand new adventures. Or I may be reminded that there is nothing I need do. All is well right where I am.

Ideas bloom and grow inside me. I am inspired!

December 10

Watching my thoughts brings me freedom. When I watch my thoughts, I can catch myself in the act of less-than-kind self-talk. The act of observing negative chatter brings me one step away from it. I can stop, regroup, and think again! As I cultivate kindness inside my head, I have less need to reach for substances to feel better. I feel better all by myself. Today, I watch my thoughts. Today, I cultivate freedom.

As I free my mind, I free myself.

December 11

Studies have shown that my attitude toward stress determines how it affects me. If I view stress negatively, it has a negative impact. If I view stress as a *positive* factor in my life, it energizes me. How about that?! Today I make friends with the stress in my life. I reframe it as energy. I reframe it as excitement. Who says stress has to be bad for me? I'm the boss of that choice!

My life rocks! My life is exciting and energizing!

December 12

Exposing my new ideas to potentially critical people is like exposing a tiny new plant to a hurricane. *Not a good idea!*

I treat my new ideas with tender loving care.

There is a time for sharing new ventures. But I also honor the need for my tiny new ideas to be nurtured before sharing them with others. And when I *do* decide it's time to share, I am extremely selective about whom I tell and how I say it. I protect my creativity and my dreams like they are my own little creativity-babies. Because they are!

I protect my tender dreams today. I nurture them tenderly.

December 13

You are made of the same Power that creates stars & planets & rocket ships.

You are a rockin' powerful being!

Everything I can see is created by one energy, one energy that fuels all of creation. Today I bask in this awareness. I think of the most powerful thing *ever*, and I remember that I am made of the same energy as *that*. I imagine myself as this super-powerful thing, and I expand my awareness of what is possible. I am powerful! I am creating an amazing life for myself and others. Today I embrace my power.

I am power. I am mighty. I am *amazing*!

December 14

Sometimes I want to quit. Sometimes everything seems too hard. But if I'm passionate about something, there's never a good reason to quit. *Never!* When I'm feeling discouraged, it's a great time to remember my original inspiring moment. The Power and Presence that got me started is still with me. Right here and right now. When I remember *that*, I pick myself up and keep going.

I remember why I started. I am renewed!

December 15

When I judge, I turn friends into monsters.

I practice releasing judgment.
It sets me free!

Judgment is no fun. Not for me, and not for the people I judge. When I judge, I am telling fractured and contracted stories about other people – and myself. On the other hand, when I let Spirit's love into my heart and mind, I view others and myself with kindness. With forgiveness. With gratitude. Today I cultivate this view. Today I let the monsters go!

I view the world with the eyes of love. What a relief!

December 16

Try Meditation.

(Unless stepping into a Technicolor Stream of Rainbow Goodness isn't for you.)
(Then never mind.)

I may not step into a Technicolor Stream of Rainbow Goodness every time I meditate. But meditation opens me to the
possibility of such experiences. It also opens me to the
opportunity to see Rainbow Goodness in my life when I'm
not meditating. After all, the animating wonder of Spirit is in
everyone and everything. Meditation is one way to tap into
this wonder. Rainbow Goodness – that's for me!

I tap into streams of Rainbow Goodness today.

December 17

When I am hanging with one of my soul peeps, I feel alive. I feel excited about life and my connection with Source. I see that I bring out the same aliveness and excitement in them. This fuels even more aliveness and excitement – a Blisscious Cycle! When one of my relationships comes to a natural end, I release attachment. I let go and open to more compatible peeps. It's a win-win for all!

I allow my relationships to be a source of inspiration.

December 18

For every conflict, there is a peaceful and loving solution.

I choose peace and love today!

Sometimes I feel the need to fight for what I believe. But fighting rarely brings peace. Today I remember that if it's peace I want, but I'm feeling upset, defensive, or combative, "I can't get there from here." I calm myself. I allow the peace that lives within me to well up, and I invite my combative feelings to surrender. I stay committed to what I really want, and I find my way to it. Love and Peace are my reward.

In the midst of conflict, I stay true to Love and Peace.

December 19

No matter what happens, I am in control of how I see it. That's why the power of positivity is so strong. When I choose to see the positive elements of everything, I unleash the positive capacities of everything. That is what I do today. I view every choice I make, and every outcome of every choice, through a lens of positivity. I also view the choices of others through this lens. What a great view!

I unleash my powers of positivity into the world today!

December 20

Sometimes I think all my problems would be solved if I had hair like Farrah Fawcett. Then I remember that her hairstyle is really out of date and would probably only make things worse. Better to just be myself!

When I look at the world around me, I see all kinds of people. Some people I'm not fond of. Others I really admire. Sometimes, when I really admire someone, it's easy to think that if I were more like them, everything in my life would be perfect. But then I would be *them*, not *me*. I am a unique, amazing creation of Spirit. If I abandon who I am and try to be someone else, I am denying Spirit's expression as *me*.

I am beautiful, unique creation of the Divine.

December 21

Who's the strongest of them all?

Work it, baby!

Is there anything stronger than peace? *Nope.* Today I rest in the power of peace. I connect with this power in my mind. I allow peace to soften my frets and anxieties. I connect with peace in my body. I consciously relax and breathe peace into every pore, every muscle, every tissue. I connect with peace in my soul. My soul *is* peace. My soul knows only peace. Today, this is all I know too.

I am peace today. It fills my mind, my body, and my soul.

December 22

When I set my intention to have an awesome day, I am more likely to have an awesome day. It's as simple as that. I can also re-set my intention at any time during the day. Today I remember to start all my endeavors and experiences with intention. Today I live a life that tickles me with its wonderful surprises. Yay life! Yay *me!*

I set my intention throughout my day. I perpetuate the *awesome***!**

December 23

Ever feel like the elephants are running your circus?

YOUR LIFE

Who's in charge of my life? I am! That's who!

The next time I think that any person or circumstance is running my life, I pause. Although I may have been caught in the illusion that someone or something else was in control, that's never the case. No matter what's going on, I am in charge of my life. There's only one power I surrender to, and that's Spirit. Not the elephants. Today I remember who's in charge. And who's not!

Spirit gives me my power. I own it today!

December 24

There are tons of angels in the world. I'm one of them.

I earn my wings today!

Every time I am kind to someone else, I am an angel. Every time I am kind to myself, I am an angel. Every time I send someone a loving thought, I am an angel. My angel capacities are endless. I share them with the world today. How can I help? How can I uplift? How can I spread joy? There are lots of answers to these questions. Today I explore them.

I am an angel. I spread some angel love today!

December 25

Love solves all my problems. When I wonder what to do, I ask, *What would Love do?* When I wonder how to handle a difficult situation, I welcome Love in. Love guides me whenever I ask it. I remember to ask today. I invite more Love into my life. I welcome It to fully express in me, as me. As I do so, I find Love everywhere I go.

I am a Love Rockstar today. I. Am. Love.

December 26

There's no such thing as doing nothing. I'm always doing *something*. Even if it's just breathing. But when I allow myself to slow down enough that my *doing* is mostly *being*, I am in a magical place. A space where rest and relaxation happens. A space where new ideas are born. A space I can come back to again and again to regroup and regenerate. Thank God for nothing!

I let myself do a whole lot of nothing.

December 27

Fashion can be a fun way to express myself. Fashion can also pull me off course, causing me to worry if what I'm wearing looks good enough. But all I have to do is smile, and I'll always look good! When I smile, I remind myself that I rock. When I smile, I bring joy to others. When I smile, I remember that there's nothing more fashionable than love. Today I share my fashionable loving smile with the world.

I smile. And the world smiles back at me!

December 28

There's nothing quite so wonderful as a good night's sleep. There's also nothing quite so wonderful as *affirming* that I get a good night's sleep. As I affirm that I sleep soundly, I allow my body to receive the message. I allow my mind to calm and slow down. As I affirm that I sleep well, night after night, my body starts to respond. I sleep deeply and peacefully. Dreamland, here I come!

I sleep soundly and deeply, night after night. Zzzzzzzz.

December 29

When I come to the end of my life, I want to know that I tried. I want to know that I went after my dreams and took chances. Given that I have no idea when my last day will be, today is the day to keep trying and taking chances. What can I do today to push the envelope a little? Or a lot?! What can I do to express my unique gifts and essence? Today I do that. Tomorrow I do that. Every day I do that!

I express myself today – fully, wildly, and completely!

December 30

Heartbreak is a part of life. Although it hurts, heartbreak is also a way to expand my capacity for love. As my heart is stretched wide open, I can let in the love of others. I can let in sweet love for myself. And I can let in the love of the Divine. Sometimes, when I'm really hurting, that's all I can do – simply sit in the pain and be open to love. And, when it comes, my open heart is ready.

I open my heart today. I open to Love.

December 31

When I'm entering a new situation, it can be scary. What's going to happen? Am I going to be okay? Am I going to have to do new things, things I don't like? When I walk by faith, not by sight, I remember the answers to these questions. No, I don't know what's going to happen, but I am going to be okay. I may need to do new things, but Spirit is with me in every step.

I embrace the new. Spirit helps me do it.

Acknowledgements

We would like to thank the Divine/The All/Source, from whence comes *everything*. We are joyously grateful every day (everyday joy!) for You. Thank you to Jill Shinn for talking us through this project, from conception to layout to editing. You are already a dear friend – now you are an invaluable resource as well. Thank you to Laura Berman for your editing eye (and awesomeness in general). Thanks to our friends and family for your love and support – you keep us going! And finally, thanks to all the folks online who encouraged us to turn the *OhMyGod Life* memes into a book. *Everyday Joy* would not exist without you.

About the Authors

Melissa and Z are both long-time students and teachers of consciousness and transformation. Over the years, they've developed unique techniques and practices for personal growth and expansion. At their virtual home-sweet-home, OhMyGodLife.com, they share their knowledge and joy in videos, classes, music, books, blogs, memes, and more. They also speak, perform, and facilitate workshops and retreats world-wide.

Both Melissa and Z hold Masters Degrees in Consciousness Studies from Holmes Institute. Melissa is also a Toltec Mentor personally trained by don Miguel Ruiz, author of *The Four Agreements*. Z also holds a Masters Degree from J.F.K. University in Spiritual Counseling Psychology.

25911730R00207

Made in the USA
Columbia, SC
08 September 2018